D1236378

Management Control Models

BASIC MANAGEMENT SERIES

GENERAL EDITORS

Huxley Madeheim
City University of New York

Edward M. Mazze
West Virginia University

Charles S. Stein
Bristol-Meyers Company

Management Control Models

EARL P. STRONG
Assistant Dean
and Professor of Management

ROBERT D. SMITH
Assistant Professor of Management
College of Business Administration
The Pennsylvania State University

HOLT, RINEHART AND WINSTON

NEW YORK   CHICAGO   SAN FRANCISCO   ATLANTA
DALLAS   MONTREAL   TORONTO   LONDON

To Mid and Vilma

Editor's Foreword

The Basic Management Series is a collection of supplementary textbooks intended for use in basic management courses, in advanced management courses at the undergraduate and graduate levels, and in executive development programs and seminars. The advantages of such a series of concise books is that they give the instructor flexibility in building a course that will expose his students to varied points of view and approaches to management as well as to current research findings. Short, supplementary books help to strengthen and bring standard management textbooks up to date. Moreover, the series introduces students to the writings of leading specialists in the field of management who have both academic and practical experience.

Each book in the series is a self-contained treatment of an important subject area in management. Three treat aspects of the management of human resources: *Organizations: Theory and Classical Concepts, The Management of Human Relations,* and *Management Control Models.* A key area of management is covered in *Manufacturing Management: An Overview.* A new area of management receiving much concern is treated in *International Management.*

The Basic Management Series is based on the idea that the practice and the study of management are changing fundamentally as a result of the accelerated rate of change in the environment surrounding management action and the explosion of knowledge in business-related disciplines. It is hoped that the books in the series will stimulate the student to study further into the field of management. It is also hoped that educators will continue to conduct and report their research findings on management.

HUXLEY MADEHEIM
EDWARD M. MAZZE
CHARLES S. STEIN

Preface

The function of management control is regarded as one of the most difficult tasks that faces the executive functioning in the modern business world. The purpose of controls is to inform the executive of how things are going—a warning, in many instances, of what is occurring, what has occurred, and what may occur if action is not taken. There is, of course, a direct tie-in with plans and objectives of the organization and the executive needs to know from time to time how results look in as objective terms as possible. The models are many and varied to give the executive the information he desires. Many of these—possibly the most useful ones—are presented in this book.

The entire process of control in an organization, from the gathering of needed information, the reporting and evaluating of the information, and the taking of corrective action, is analogous to a thermostat. The thermostat is set for a certain limit and, when that limit is reached, the thermostat automatically reports it and the mechanism activates the equipment to correct the situation until a desired result is achieved. The corrective action, however, in an actual business situation is not always automatic. Decisions need to be reached by executives and corrective action taken when necessary. One of the features of this book is its basic approach to the decision process.

The system of control that is used in any given situation depends largely upon the objectives of the organization and the amount and type of information required for decision-making. It is important, therefore, that whatever system or part of a system is used be effective and achieve the required results. Control is essential to the success of any enterprise.

Acknowledgment is given to a number of persons who contributed material, ideas, and suggestions that have made this book more useful than it otherwise would have been. These persons are: Dr. John J. Willingham, Associate Professor of Accounting, the Pennsylvania State University, and Mr. Robert A. Olsen, Associate Professor of Industrial Engineering, the Pennsylvania State University. Also, grateful acknowledgment is extended to the several publishers who gave permission to use material and quotations from their publications and to W. C. Heath and Associates, Milwaukee, Wisconsin, for permission to use a Cartogram from their collection of business control charts.

Grateful recognition is also given to Mrs. Eva T. Burke, who so capably prepared the manuscript for publication.

EARL P. STRONG

ROBERT D. SMITH

University Park, Pennsylvania
July 1968

Contents

Management Control Models

CHAPTER ONE

Principles of Control

Introduction

One of the most persistent problems facing an executive is that of *control*. Managers of business, political, social, military, and religious organizations are daily confronted with complicated decisions regarding the acquisition and use of human and material resources. The purpose of this book is to provide leaders of today, as well as those of tomorrow, with selective techniques which can be used for better executive control.

This chapter contains an explanation of a general control system and the principles an executive should keep in mind if he wishes his control system to be effective. Other chapters are devoted to specific guides for the control of organization, finances, personnel, and information.

There are a number of conflicting viewpoints regarding the best manner in which to manage an organization. However, theorists as well as practicing executives agree that *good management requires effective control*. A combination of well-planned objectives, strong organization, capable direction, and motivation have little probability for success unless there exists an adequate system of control.

Consider the situation of a subordinate saying to his superior, "But, sir, I didn't know that our raw material supply was below the safety stock level; my status reports were not totaled. I'm sorry we weren't able to fill the order on time." Had you been the president of a growing enterprise, which had just lost a large order and a good customer, would you have accepted this explanation from your production supervisor? Your first inclination might have been to discharge him; or, more rationally, you might have developed additional facts before taking such drastic action. The first question that could be asked is, "Who was responsible for this unfortunate event?" More precisely, however, you should ask "Who had *control* over the situation?" Certainly, someone, somewhere within the firm knew that materials were in dangerously short supply and, if this assumption is valid, it must be determined why the information did not reach the proper destination in time to prevent a grave imbalance within the organization.

The above example of operational control failure illustrates the proposition that the essence of control is *information* which is communicated effectively and efficiently throughout the organizational system.[1] Other important factors which must be considered pertaining to control are: planning, standards, measurement, and corrective action. Each of these, however, has something in common with the others: none is of value or even meaningful without significant, accurate, timely, and well-communicated information.

Definition of Control

The United States serves as the hub of a technologically explosive world society. The corporate executive who wishes to manage his organization successfully must be able to recognize and understand the dynamic nature of the system in which his business functions. Just as a thermostat reacts to variations in the physical environment, so must the modern manager sense and respond to changes within his company. *Control* is a function through which the

---

[1] The term *system* as used in this book is defined as a group of interrelated elements placed together for the purpose of obtaining an objective common to each element. In accordance with accepted terminology, each system comprises the following components: inputs, outputs, transformations, memory, and feedback.

executive is able to identify change, discover its causes, and provide decisive action in order to maintain a state of equilibrium within the system for which he has managerial responsibility and authority.

Von Bertalanfy, a pioneer in general systems theory, states that science no longer seeks to discover and control through mere analysis and isolation of particular elements or components.[2] Rather, he claims that it is necessary to think in terms of systems of elements in mutual interaction. The systems approach, adopted in this book, thus provides an integrated frame of reference for anlyzing internal *and* external factors related to the control of an enterprise. Hereafter, the organization is viewed as a system (internal) comprised of various business subsystems, such as production, marketing, finance, engineering and others. The system is considered "adaptive," as it is capable of reacting to changes in the economic, social, political, and technological environment (external system) in which it operates.

Information fed into a managerial control center, human or computer, serves as a storage element until there is sufficient evidence to render a decision. Thus the control center is responsible for taking appropriate follow-up action to assure that the decision has been implemented.

Before the age of mass production, specialization, and decentralization, the chief executive knew his employees, his suppliers, and even his customers on an individual basis. He learned the capabilities of his people and equipment. Functioning on his own, he was able to plan, organize, and control his daily operations. He was able to stay abreast of his problems and usually resolved them without resorting to complicated techniques of analysis. But just as the small business of yesterday has evolved into the organizational system of today, so also have decision problems, related to the control of these systems, grown more complex. No longer can a decision be made without first thinking about its effects on other areas of the firm as well as upon other firms in the industry. Today, there is critical need for faster and better information in order to maintain control of operations.

To summarize, the purpose of control is to provide the business system with effective information, decision rules, and means to take corrective action in such a way as to attain objectives. Control is used to regulate the organization and maintain a state of equilibrium which is dynamic (adaptive) and sensitive to changes both within as well

---

[2] Ludwig von Bertalanfy, "General Systems Theory," *General Systems,* vol. 1, 1956, p. 56.

as outside the "company walls." Control is the final action phase of the manager who has properly planned, structured, staffed, and delegated.

Cost of Control

Much has been written about those energetic but unfortunate entrepreneurs who have controlled themselves into bankruptcy because they felt a need to oversee everything and everyone within their organization. This approach to control is usually as unfavorable as too little control and becomes most burdensome and expensive. What should be established are points of strategic control whereby standards are set in only those processes vital to the successful operation of the business. When these points are identified, management is by *exception* through directing energies to the processes that demonstrate ineffective performance rather than to those that are running smoothly.

Normally, the business enterprise should extend its controls only until the marginal costs of additional control are equal to the incremental cost savings resulting from the control. When analyzing the cost of a control system, opportunity losses of personnel and equipment should not be overlooked. For example, data processing equipment might be more effectively utilized in the resolving of line balancing problems rather than in the maintenance of routine daily inventory records. When industrial engineers are used to solve production line problems, where computerized techniques have already been developed to perform this task, the time of these people must be considered when evaluating the cost of the inventory control system. Of course, such opportunity costs become significant only if the firm had previously been using its data processing equipment at full capacity.

Certain functions within the organizational system are more important to the welfare of the system than are others. The executive's task is to specify those that are critical and regulate them to the degree necessary to obtain desired results. Total observation and measurement, even within critical areas, is rarely necessary. Sample results which are selected, measured, analyzed, and immediately reported are usually sufficient to reflect accurately the state of a system. By establishing strategic points of control and then sampling performance on a regular basis at these points, control costs can be reduced.

As an example of this approach, consider the reactions of the president of a dress manufacturing plant who one day is informed that sales have fallen 25 percent from the previous month. Immediately he visits a sample of his most important customers in an attempt to find a reason for the sudden loss of interest in his product. A summary of the replies shows that the customers are dissatisfied because new styles were late in arriving at their retail destinations.

On returning to the plant, the chief executive contacts his production superintendent and requests an explanation. The subordinate explains that he is maintaining a policy of holding orders for large batch production so as to reduce his overall operating expenditures. The president, feeling that he has reached the heart of the problem, issues a decision rule for new orders, stating that no order is to be held longer than four days. Further, he installs a reporting system to provide immediate feedback on the number, size, priority, dates, and production progress of all orders.

Did this action resolve the problems of declining sales due to customer dissatisfaction over delivery? Unfortunately, it did not. The reason for the unresponsiveness of the system to the seemingly appropriate corrective action was due to other strategic processes within the organization which had been contributing to the problem. The president had not looked far enough; he had not conducted a systems analysis. If he had looked further, he would have discovered that his salesmen were promising unrealistic delivery dates in order to obtain greater initial sales; that the shipping department was allowing finished goods to stockpile for more efficient utilization of carrier space; and that administrative assistants were picking up the daily mail an hour before schedule and thereby missing a large portion of a day's order volume. In addition, inventory control personnel were not familiar with supplier lead times which meant that raw material inventories were subject to out-of-stock conditions at critical periods. All or any one of these subsystem elements could have been the cause of late delivery and customer dissatisfaction.

This firm lacked an effective analysis of all subsystem operating procedures and subsequent development of a control network which integrated information flows among organization elements. The term "rhocrematics" has been coined to describe the interaction of material and information flows within the total system which includes the firm, its suppliers, and its customers. For a full discussion of the dynamic interrelationships which take place within the business organization, the reader may wish to refer to the book *Industrial Dynamics*.[3]

The Control Cycle

One of the most widely accepted approaches to managerial control involves the closed-loop model shown in Figure 1-1. This model

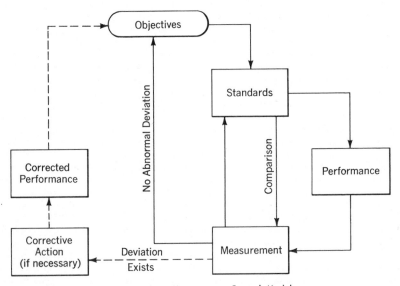

Figure 1-1   Management Control Model

begins with the establishment of objectives for the organization and completes its cycle with their attainment. Between the time goals are set and reached, important managerial functions take place. The control function requires that standards of performance be developed in those strategic elements which affect the attainment of the objectives. Then performance must be measured to determine whether or not it meets the standards. If performance is found to be outside acceptable limits of variation from standard, corrective action leading toward the attainment of objectives is necessary. Thus, the reader notes how the model resembles a closed cycle of control, beginning

---

[3] J. W. Forrester, *Industrial Dynamics*. New York: John Wiley and Sons, 1961.

and ending with corporate objectives. It should be pointed out that each phase of the cycle is important and, if one element is overlooked, control is apt to be lacking within the system. We will now treat separately each of the elements of the control cycle.

Objectives

Without objectives, there are no criteria for evaluating performance and, in fact, there is no real need for managment. Without the minimum goal of mere survival, an organization could be left to flounder until it finally dissolved. Objectives are the first phase of the managerial control cycle shown in Figure 1-1.

Where should objectives be set? Many managers feel that as long as they set a profit goal and reach it, the firm is successful. This may be true in the short run, but the question arises as to how long a firm will be successful if it seeks only to maximize its profits. Peter Drucker says that objectives should be established for every area that vitally affects the survival of the enterprise. He lists these areas as market share, research and development, productivity, physical and financial resources, managerial and worker performance, and public responsibility. If one were to set reasonable short- and long-range objectives in each of these areas and subsequently reach them, there is little doubt as to the probable success of the enterprise.

When one drives an automobile, the direction taken is determined by the objective set—the destination desired. Speed is also determined by the objective. If the objective is to enjoy a weekend trip to a cabin in the country, a leisurely pace of 40 miles per hour may be set; if the objective is to rush an injured person to the hospital, the speed will be greater. Of course, environmental factors, such as bad weather, heavy traffic, or motorcycle patrolmen, may prevent or delay one from reaching his objective but these are elements over which the person has no control. The point is that a car is controlled by an individual who in turn is controlled by his objectives and environmental circumstances. Without an objective in mind, therefore, one might drive aimlessly without direction until running out of gasoline or becoming lost. The same thing can happen to the business firm that does not set and publicize its objectives—it wanders about until it runs out of capital or is consumed by its competition.

Thus, the first criteria for effective control is the development and communication of goals which provide a common direction within the organization. These objectives should be realistic and challenging, yet attainable. They should be expressed as quantitatively as possible (so they can be measured) and in terms which can be easily understood, such as ratios, dollars, turnover rates, or time periods. General objectives, such as to increase sales, cut processing time, or speed up cash flow, are not sufficient. Objectives should be stated more precisely, such as to increase sales by 15 percent within the next year, to lower manufacturing cycle time to three hours, or to raise capital turnover to one and one-half times its present rate within six months.

To establish objectives for the firm as a whole is not sufficient either. All managers and employees within the firm should establish individual objectives, which, if attained, would contribute to the achievement of the overall objectives of the enterprise. Integration of personal and organization goals reduces conflicts and dissatisfaction and helps to eliminate those compromising situations where a manager or employee is forced to choose between his personal aspirations and the best interests of the organization. A specific example will help to clarify this point.

Dan Brown is manager of the Radar Simulator Division of Simtec Electronics, Inc., a highly decentralized manufacturing corporation where each division manager is evaluated on the basis of the particular product for which he has responsibility. Richard Teel, a bright young supervisor on Brown's assembly line, has demonstrated exceptional executive potential and is being considered for a promotion as head of a newly-organized Management Information Department at corporate staff level. Brown does not want to lose Teel's exceptional abilities and, consequently, turns in a low efficiency report at the time of the annual employee appraisals. As a result, an outsider is brought in to fill the vacant staff position.

In this situation, the firm as a whole probably suffered because the better man was not placed at the head of the staff department. The Radar Division is likely to be better off although this is questionable, especially if Teel realized what had happened.

In the above example, Mr. Brown is being evaluated on the basis of product performance and, consequently, does not want to part with a good production supervisor. If Simtec's top management had recognized management development as another criterion for evaluating performance, Brown would probably have seen that his young supervisor received an honest appraisal and promotion. What the Radar Division manager failed to accept was that what was good for the firm was good for himself. Situations such as the above occur in those firms where the goals of an individual do not match the goals of the organization of which the individual is a part. What can be done to prevent similar instances from arising? Unfortunately, human nature being as variable as it is, there are no organizational "tonics" which can be given to cure the illness. A good point to keep in mind in this respect, however, is that managers should never be evaluated on the basis of a single criterion, such as profitability, return on investment, or operating efficiency. This type of evaluation system often leads a manager to seek short-run objectives at the expense of the long-run welfare of the firm.

Another example of the dangers of a single objective criteria for evaluating performance occurred at the Texas Instruments Company[4] in the early 1960s. A product manager was told that he would be evaluated on the basis of the return on assets for his division. When a quarterly report indicated that his return was below the objective established for him by top management, he considered following one of three courses of action in order to improve his immediate position. These alternatives were: (1) to reduce advertising even though he knew it would have a long-run unfavorable effect on sales; (2) to reduce raw material inventories knowing that a danger of being out of stock would exist; and (3) to prolong the hiring of two additional engineers even though they would be critically required for the development of new products. This manager, obviously, was influenced by short-run considerations at the expense of the long-run welfare of the firm. It should be noted that the firm recognized its managerial mistakes and has since altered its evaluation system.

Standards

The second phase of the managerial control cycle (see Figure 1-1) is the development of realistic standards of performance. A standard is defined as a minimum level of output expected of everyone working within the system. A large amount of planning is usually required if the standards are to be meaningful. The planners must consider not only the internal operations of the firm but also trends in the economy, advances in technology, activities of competitors, and preferences of the consumer when instituting performance standards. It certainly would be unrealistic to establish high quality standards

---

[4] E. P. Learned, C. R. Christensen, K. R. Andrews, and D. Guth, *Business Policy*. Homewood, Ill.: Richard D. Irwin, Inc., 1965, pp. 705–706.

with exacting tolerances if the consumer were interested in a low cost, medium quality item.

Standard setting also requires a systems approach. For example, it would be questionable practice for the sales force to promise a maximum two-week delivery time when the production department requires ten days merely to set up for a new run. If potential customers were able to get faster delivery from competitors, it would probably be necessary to reevaluate the entire system and perhaps revise the company standards pertaining to the maintenance of final inventories.

Once the planners have examined the external system (the general economy, technology, competitors, and consumers), they must look at the firm itself in relation to its environment to determine the effects of the standards they set on the internal system.[5] For instance, if a two-day lead time for customer delivery were to be set, would the inspection, packaging, and shipping departments be capable of complying without excessive strain upon their respective resources? Or, if we raise our acceptable outgoing quality level to 4 percent from its present 3 percent (meaning that four rather than three items out of every 100 leaving the plant could be defective), would the marketing and public relations functions be confronted with overly burdensome customer complaints and possible loss of business? Certainly, one could lower inspection costs and perhaps engineering costs by allowing a wider range of tolerance, but the question arises as to how this new standard would influence the remainder of the system. In order to determine the effects of proposed standards upon the *total* system, it is necessary first to divide the firm into its component parts or elements (analysis) and then to place these parts in proper corporate and environmental perspective (synthesis).

The manager must know what has happened in the past within the firm and, if possible, what has taken place in other firms which operate in the same industry. Accurate records can provide management with a store of relevant information which, if properly updated and utilized, are an invaluable assistance in maintaining effective control. For example, if it is desired to set a standard personnel turnover rate of 10 percent, one should determine what the turnover rate has been in previous years, what the rate is for competitors, what the rate

---

[5] Assuming the firm is established along normal functional lines, the elements of the internal system would probably be the basic organic functions of finance, marketing, and production as a minimum with such other elements as personnel or engineering as determined by individual company needs.

is for the industry as a whole, and, finally, the condition of the current labor market.

When establishing control standards, it is important to bear in mind the fact that some degree of variation is inherent in every industrial process or administrative operation. It is unlikely that two drilled holes will have exactly the same diameter to ten-thousandths of an inch nor should it be expected that the office secretary makes the same number of mistakes for every ten pages she types. Variation in performance may be microscopically small and seemingly insignificant, but it does exist and must be provided for when standards are developed. The natural variation in a process due to differences in people, material, and machinery is classified as "normal."

The question is: How much variation is allowable before it can no longer be considered normal? To cope with this phenomenon of natural variation, we need to establish upper and lower limits of acceptable variation. If a measured result exceeds either of these limits, a very high probability exists that variation has gone beyond what might normally be expected if a system were in control. For example, a manufacturing plant might have historical data indicating that the average accident rate over the past three years was seven a month with a standard deviation of one accident a month. If it can be assumed that the number of accidents a month follows a normal pattern of distribution, common statistical practice is followed in the establishment of upper and lower control limits of three standard deviations from the average. This means that if there were eleven accidents in a given month, a high probability exists that the accident rate is no longer normal and a signal flashes to management that an assignable cause for this excessive variation should be sought. Or, this information might be used to test the effectiveness of a safety campaign by observing the lower limit of the control system, which is calculated by subtracting three standard deviations from the mean. If one were to observe that the accident rate for a month during which safety was "pushed" was two, we could be relatively certain that the reduced number of accidents was not due to normal circumstances since it was less than the average minus the three standard deviations $(7 - 3 = 4)$. The conclusion would be that the safety campaign probably had some effect upon the accident rate. Discussion of the concepts of statistical control, normal distribution, and standard deviation is beyond the scope and purpose of this book. However, it is a vital phase of managerial control and those readers who are not familiar with these basic statistical tools may wish to refer to an introductory statistics book, such as the one mentioned in the footnote below.[6]

One final note pertaining to standards which is important to keep in mind is the idea of "double standards." It has been found that output varies in both quantity and quality from one shift to another. Thus, consideration should be given to varying the standards between shifts or even between the same shift on different days. Industrial planners at General Motors discovered the unusual phenomenon that employee performance was different on Monday than it was on the other working days and, consequently, set different performance standards for the first working day of the week. The reader might guess that the activities of the weekend played an important role in determining the level of performance exhibited immediately following.

Measure of Performance

The third stage of the managerial control cycle involves measurement of performance to determine whether or not the standards have been met. If performance does fall within the preestablished control limits, there is a high probability that the system is under control. An important point should be raised here. Many executives fall into a trap when they assume that, because they are meeting standards, everything is fine. The executive should be on the alert to detect changes in the internal or external system which require re-evaluation of standards. For example, the organization which sets a standard rejection rate of 5 percent might find that after the purchase of new equipment this figure should be lowered to 4 percent.

Effective measurement of performance requires that the executive determine the type of management information which he needs from each of the strategic elements within his area of responsibility. Information becomes his key to control. He must identify those points within his area of responsibility which affect the attainment of his goals and then see that significant, timely, relevant, and accurate factual data are gathered and communicated through a streamlined information feedback network. This action must be performed on a regular and formal basis. Unnecessary delays in the feedback network will cause distortion and lead to erratic fluctuations in the balance of the system. For example, consider a three-stage distribution

---

[6] N. M. Downie and R. W. Heath, *Basic Statistical Methods.* New York: Harper and Row, Publishers, 1965, pp. 18–60.

system comprised of a factory warehouse, wholesalers, and retailers. If there were a delay in reporting heavy increases in demand at the retail level, a firm's production facilities might not be able to re-supply its wholesalers in sufficient time to satisfy this demand and, consequently, lose a sizable amount of sales.

One of the most recent innovations in information technology is that of real-time analysis, which allows management to base its control decisions on up-to-date data gathered from all strategic areas of operation. Computerized retrieval systems relay day-to-day pro-duction, sales, and financial facts to a central memory bank which accumulates, integrates, and evaluates these facts for decision pur-poses. No longer can executives rely upon historically outdated standards for control. When competition has access to real-time in-formation, the firm should have access to the same type of informa-tion or suffer the results of falling behind in technology. More will be mentioned about computerized control methods in a later chapter.

A critical problem related to the measurement of employee per-formance is the natural tendency of men to concentrate their maxi-mum efforts in that area on which their performance will be evalu-ated. As more and more emphasis is placed on a particular criterion of performance by top management, so will middle and lower level managers begin to be concerned primarily with this same criterion and very often at the expense of other important areas of the system.

There is an important social concept which pertains to this dis-cussion of performance measurement. In the late 1920s, a group of behavioral researchers at the Hawthorne Electric Works in Chicago recognized the phenomenon of group dynamics. They found that within the formal organization structure and its lines of authority there normally exists an informal type of group pressure which leads individuals to conform to the wishes of the informal group. Social norms are developed within the group which may or may not agree with the standards established by the company. These social norms become the "accepted" way of doing things, and if individuals do not wish to follow the norms, they are either coerced by or excluded from the informal group. Since most men have a basic need to belong to a social group of some type, the informal group plays an important role in satisfying this need, because the large and usually cold formal organization is not capable of providing this sense of belonging. As a result, men are often disinclined to behave in such a way as to cause exclusion from their circle of friends. In this way, the informal group plays an important part in determining whether or not official standards will be met. Additional research has shown that a company is most likely to reach its goals when formal and informal standards are integrated through management-worker participation. Workers (or perhaps their immediate supervisors) can be called in to discuss standards before they are set, in order that they will feel that they have played some part, as minor as it may be, in their development.

An important question which must be asked when attempting to design a control system is: Are the measurements going to be reported to management in meaningful form? For example, information that a corporation experienced only four grievances per one thousand workers per month might appear favorable and unexceptional to management, whereas the real situation was quite significant. A more complete analysis of the data might have shown that a particular department within a major division was responsible for three out of every four of the grievances. On the basis of the "average" results, management probably would feel no need for action, whereas the more detailed evaluation would indicate a need for inquiry.

Thus, it is essential that managers realize the importance of not only the methods used in measuring but also the methods used in reporting information. Every effort must be made to assure that significant data are not misrepresented.

Peter Drucker points out that 90 percent of the volume of a business is usually represented by 2 to 5 percent of the number of its products. But 90 percent of the orders by number typically covers only 4 to 5 percent of the volume yet accounts for 90 percent and more of the costs.[7]

A large aircraft may have 500,000 parts, but 90 percent of its cost might be represented by only 100 of these parts. Ninety percent of a company's distributors may account for only 20 percent of sales, while the other 10 percent moves 80 percent of the goods. Traditional accounting systems tend to conceal these critical elements of information[8] and consequently, a manager must constantly be aware of the distortions which can arise due to accurately measured but poorly presented information. Be most wary, for example, of assigning the majority of good salesmen to 70 percent of the customers who together only purchase 30 percent of the products!

Relevant to the preceding discussion is a very useful control tech-

---

[7] Peter Drucker, "Information, Control and Management," *Proceedings of the International Management Congress.* New York: Council for International Progress in Management, Inc., 1963, pp. 209–213.

[8] Drucker, p. 211.

nique often referred to as "Pareto's Law." [9] This generalized approach to control is named after the Italian economist and mathematician, Vilfredo Pareto, who discovered in 1897 a significant relationship between national income and population. Pareto found that a very large proportion of income was attributed to only a small percentage of the total population. The reader can rightfully ask how this discovery related to managerial control. The query is simply answered by saying that Pareto's Law has a much more general definition than the one expressed by national income and population relationships. What this law states is that "the significant elements in a specified group usually constitute a relatively small portion of the total items in the group." [10]

Pareto's relationship was first applied as a management technique in the area of inventory control after World War II when it was found that as little as 15 to 25 percent of a company's inventory accounted for as much as 90 percent of the total dollar value of that inventory. Later observations have indicated other areas of management susceptible to this phenomenon. For example, a firm might find that 10 percent of its employees accounts for 80 percent of its grievances; that 5 percent of its customers makes 90 percent of its complaints; that 90 percent of its orders comes from 5 percent of its clients, and so forth.

If these types of relationships are recognized by management, a more efficient and effective control system can be developed. It seems logical that a company would not allocate its inspection personnel equally throughout its manufacturing operations. It is more reasonable to apply the greatest quality control efforts in those parts of the system where the effects of poor quality are likely to cause the greatest amount of harm. Items with low dollar value, low rework cost, or with wide tolerances would most likely receive less attention than those items with critical design characteristics, rigid tolerances, or high replacement costs. This reasoning is very logical but it is surprising to note that very little consideration is given to this concept by either the federal government or industrial quality control planners.[11]

What in effect is being said is that standard, company-wide control systems do not always make the best use of organization re-

[9] C. J. Slaybaugh, "Pareto's Law and Modern Management," *Price Waterhouse Review* XI, no. 4 (Winter 1966), pp. 26–33.

[10] Slaybaugh, p. 27.

[11] Robert D. Smith, "Quality Assurance in Government and Industry: A Bayesian Approach," *Journal of Industrial Engineering*, May 1966, pp. 254–259.

sources. Management should apply its effort in the area where it will do the most good. Executives must identify the significant factors in a given operation, concentrate their control on these factors, and leave the less important areas of control to subordinates or in some cases permit these factors to "control themselves" through the Exception Principle.

The general shape of a Pareto curve is shown in Figure 1-2. Such

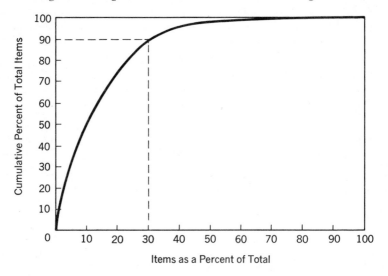

Figure 1-2 Pareto Curve

a curve can be approximated for many managerial problems and will show the executive where the significant items of a group constitute a relatively small percentage of the total group. Once the general shape of the curve is established, the executive can determine a point on the curve up to which maximum control should be exerted. For example, if the curve in Figure 1-2 indicates that 30 percent of the tools used by a firm accounted for 90 percent of the total value of all the tools used by the firm, a special tool crib might be constructed to control the 30 percent of valuable items while the remainder might be charged out to the individual workmen.

Corrective Action

When measurement indicates that the firm or one of its elements is not operating within the established standards, the control process has performed its function of identifying abnormal variation. In this case, management should have a contingency plan which will lead to the elimination of the excessive variance from standard by directing resources toward those areas where performance is inadequate. This is the final phase of the control cycle shown in Figure 1-1, that of corrective action.

Control standards are developed for those individuals who have responsibility for a particular element within the total organizational system. Responsibility accounting is probably one of the best methods of identifying which manager should be "corrected" if standards are not being achieved. Under this procedure managers who can control certain expenditures are identified and held personally accountable for them. Thus, organization for control is often decentralized. Psychologically, it is easier to implement corrective action if a line supervisor can be shown that his section (rather than his whole department) is responsible for a serious deviation from standard. It should be remembered, however, that for good control, a clear division should be made between operating responsibility and the accounting for the execution of that responsibility.

General Characteristics of the Control Cycle

In addition to the specific principles mentioned with regard to each phase of the control cycle shown in Figure 1-1, the following general principles apply to the control system as a whole.

Flexibility. Controls must be developed which allow adaptation to individual situations and changes in the organizational environment. If, for example, the price of raw steel is suddenly increased, direct material standards should be altered to reflect this price change. Also, workers' attitudes will be adversely affected if standards are so rigid that they do not fit local conditions. Flexible budgets provide a type of sliding scale which increases or decreases with variations in product output, and therefore contribute to the maintenance of employee morale.

Consistency. Controls must be identified as consistent with company objectives and policies. A firm, for example, which has established an objective to develop a quality image should not require extremely high standards in its television division and allow poor workmanship in its radio division.

Clarity. Controls must be written and communicated so that everyone who is affected by them from top management to production line workers can understand them.

Immediate Feedback. Deviations from standard should be reported as soon as possible, the optimum being real-time feedback.

Discretionary Corrective Action. Corrective action should be used only when necessary and, when taken, decisions should be firm and reasonable.

Unlimited use of the "red flag" will tend to build a feeling of apathy on the part of employees toward controls.

Pervasiveness. Control should exist at all levels within the organization. First line supervisors find it difficult to react to a system which controls only lower echelons while higher levels operate in an atmosphere of laxity.

Summary

If progress toward goals is to be controlled, observation and measurement of performance are required. Measurement indicates where the system or one of its components is compared with where it ought to be. To state where a system ought to be is to set a standard. Standards, in turn, are based upon the objectives desired. Thus, it is clear that each part of the control cycle is directly related and dependent upon the preceding phase of the cycle.

The normal reasons for lack of control within a business firm can be classified into four general categories.

1. Objectives are not specifically defined and communicated in writing to those within the organization who are responsible for attaining them.

2. Objectives are unrealistic, either too difficult or too easy to attain.

3. Established policies and procedures are not being complied with.

4. Programs designed for the various functional areas (marketing, production, finance, for example) are not integrated into a coordinated systems framework.

Effective control must be accompanied by careful and integrated planning which views the organization as a system of interrelated functions, each with specific authority and responsibility. Control points must be located strategically within the firm so that relevant information is generated and swiftly transmitted to a destination where it can be analyzed, evaluated, and interpreted for decision purposes.

A sound executive control system provides information, evaluates this information, gauges actual performance against established plans, and finally assures that corrective action is taken when performance is not directed toward the achievement of organization goals.

CHAPTER TWO

Organization Control— The Staff Role

Importance of Staff

Hardly any organization of size exists which does not make wide use of staff. The size of staff relative to line organization is growing rapidly, particularly in those industries characterized by advanced technology, such as electronics and data processing. In one midwestern division of a large aircraft and missile company, 50 percent of all employees, including managerial and operative, are engaged in staff activities. In some organizations, the percentage is even greater. Since staff personnel provide much of the information required for executive control, this chapter has been devoted to those principles and techniques required to maintain an effective staff.

Several reasons exist for this phenomenal growth in the size and importance of corporate staffs. One of the primary explanations is that the present era is witnessing an astronomical increase in the amount of knowledge available to man. Educators estimate that the amount of information existing in the world in 1700 was doubled by the beginning of the twentieth century; that this figure was again doubled between 1900 and 1950; and, amazing as it may seem, the amount of knowledge existing in 1950 was doubled by 1960. With such an increase in knowledge, is it any wonder that men are required to become more specialized in their field of study? Lest the reader become discouraged by such overwhelming statistics, the authors hasten to add that the same technology which is causing the knowledge explosion is also contributing to a solution. Advanced data processing and information retrieval systems will eventually allow the human intellect immediate access to stores of medical, legal, and governmental information. However, these days are still in the future and, for the present, managers will have to rely on staffs to provide guidance and answers.

Some observers refer to this period as the age of research and innovation—the research revolution. Consequently, demand exists for highly qualified specialists in technical and scientific fields, such as systems engineering, operations research, and management information retrieval.

In today's industrial complex, the work of the technician is not limited to product research and development. Mathematicians are engaged in the development of scientific approaches to managerial decision-making, which is rapidly replacing intuition as the major basis of executive judgment. Time-shared computer systems make it possible for small firms to process large quantities of information more efficiently than before. While such technological advances have replaced certain employees, they have increased at the same time the demand for more staff specialists to design, program, operate, and maintain complex new equipment.

Government and legal regulations have increased, thereby creating a need for additional staff personnel. The scope of union bargaining calls for experts in labor relations as well as in the areas of insurance and pension funding.

The staff role in organization has always been a source of problems and misunderstanding. Many firms have been able to function without understanding the nature of staff work and its relation to the rest of the organization. But today competitive business practices compel a company to know the role its staff plays in its operations.

Staff Objectives

Staff objectives are more easily defined than implemented. The prime objective of staff is to help the line organization achieve *its* goals more efficiently and effectively. This means recommending and sometimes implementing procedures to cut costs, recommending policies and programs designed to help managers cope with human relations problems, and bringing special knowledge and skills to bear for more effective long- and short-range planning.

Is our staff achieving its goals? Effective staff control functions are reflected in the reduction of substandard quality, the meeting of schedules, and keeping costs in line. But the results of staff work are not measured so easily. How can it be ascertained that a management training program is followed by more effective management performance? And even when this does happen, how can it be determined with certitude that the training program was the real cause of better performance?

Since results cannot always be measured directly, it is often necessary to evaluate staff performance by inference. Personnel work is a good example. A measure is taken of something that seems to be related and can be quantified; lower turnover, less absenteeism, and fewer grievances possibly indicate more effective personnel policies. Lower costs may infer better planning which can be attributed to staff assistance.

There are occasions when staff objectives are not firmly established or understood. Examples can be found in engineering departments which grow so large and autonomous that the relationship between their objectives and the primary product and service objectives of the firm became almost nonexistent. There have been many evidences of staff "empire building," which in itself was paradoxical to the staff's reason for existence—more efficient and effective achievement of the firm's primary product and service objectives.

Even though staff work cannot be measured with any degree of precision, a clear statement and understanding of its objectives can in itself provide a bench mark for evaluating its contribution.

Development of Staff

To understand how the staff function develops, let us examine this hypothetical illustration.

The Ajax Company is a small firm manufacturing a variety of home and gardening tools, such as tongs, rakes, and shovels. The company is owned and operated by a person whose training and experience has been in the field of mechanical engineering. His firm is presently a simple line organization, as shown in Figure 2-1.

The company has 60 employees including the owner who is

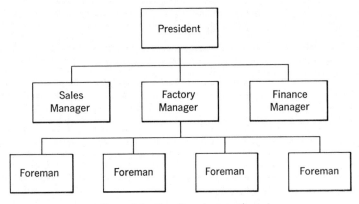

Figure 2-1   Line Organization Chart

president. Under the present structure, *all* 60 employees are in the line organization; that is, they are all engaged directly in the production, selling, and financial activities of the firm.[1]

Until the present time, this structure has been sufficient. But problems are beginning to arise. The president finds himself overburdened with activities. He designs the products himself and works out specification changes with his production supervisors. He is increasingly involved with personnel details, maintaining such governmental programs as social security and workmen's compensation for his employees. Although he has delegated the authority to hire new employees to his subordinates, he is still called upon to make the final decisions.

When the situation finally becomes impossible, the president decides he must have help to relieve himself of some of this burden. Since most of the functions he contemplates turning over to a new employee are in the personnel field, he decides to establish the position of personnel director.

The major duties of the new man will be to maintain personnel records, and to recruit and screen job applicants. The final selection will be made by line managers. The personnel director also will be expected to advise the president on matters dealing with all aspects of manpower, such as personal relations problems, training, and management development. However, the small size of the organiza-

---

[1] There is some disagreement among researchers in the field of management regarding the classification of the finance function as line or staff. While some see it as a staff operation, more generally it is conceded to be line on the basis that finance is one of the organic functions which must be performed by an enterprise.

tion will make these activities occasional. For example, the personnel director's role in training might be merely to suggest that certain line managers be sent to special conferences and workshops conducted by local schools and professional groups.

But a new development causes the director's role to be modified. A national union succeeds in organizing the operative employees. Feeling quite inept in the field of labor relations, the president relies on his personnel director to negotiate and administer the labor contract although he, himself, must give final approval to the company's agreement. This simple case situation illustrates how a staff position evolves and the basic types of work performed by a staff specialist.

Counsel and Service for Organization Control

In another organizational setting, the staff man's prime function is to provide special counsel and perform a service function for various members of the organization. For example, an industrial engineer might be hired by a small firm to establish time standards, redesign the layout of the production facilities, maintain statistical quality control data, and suggest improvements in work methods. In such a case, the staff assistant has direct working relations with the production supervisors, personnel administrator, and perhaps the cost accountant. It is most difficult in this type of situation for the staff assistant to carry out his assignments unless he possesses and exercises some form of "authority" in his specialized fields. He might show the production foreman a dangerously increasing trend in the rate of product rejection, but the foreman might ignore the advice of the staff assistant if he does not possess authority. Under these circumstances, the concept of "staff authority" becomes confusing unless it is understood and controlled.

Functional Authority Control

Functional authority is different than the service activity performed by executive assistants. The distinction between the two, however, is often not clear, thus resulting in conflicts and misunderstandings within the organization. If a staff man is delegated functional authority by the chief line executive, he is actually given the responsibility to perform a specific function or functions. On the other hand, if he is part of a service facility he performs the same function but, presumably, only when his service is requested by a lower line activity. In the instance of functional authority, the staff man does not wait for the request of lower level executives, but performs his duties when and if they become necessary. He has authority to perform his functions on his own initiative. This authority is granted him by the line executive to whom he reports. In effect, functional authority is really an extension of the line executive's authority.

The personnel director, in the example above, had the authority to perform certain well-defined functions, including negotiation and administration of labor agreements. The task of recruiting and screening new employees can be viewed as a service function. It is also an example of functional authority possessed by the personnel director, since he does not have to wait for the request of lower level line executives to initiate the procedure.

Other examples of the exercise of functional authority by staff departments are often found in engineering and cost control. In many cases, the engineering department is given authority to require compliance with design specifications for products that members of the department have determined necessary. In other instances, budgetary specialists who are classified as staff have the authority to ask for and obtain financial data from any line manager in the organization.

The exercise of functional authority is closely related to the area of procedures. In fact, functional authority is often classified as procedural authority. The staff manager who has functional authority almost always becomes involved with organizational procedures. His functional authority really means authority to develop and implement certain types of procedures. The personnel manager, for example, might develop personnel procedures for which he is able to demand compliance. The design engineer develops procedures when he decides which specifications will be followed in manufacturing a product. (The engineer is not always given complete authority and often is required to negotiate with other functional departments, such as production and marketing.)

Control Authority

The idea of functional authority can be carried one step further to include *control* authority. That is, a staff department is delegated authority to effect the compliance of procedures of all types including those not developed by itself. This work may be described as essentially "policing" procedures.

A staff department having this type of control authority can require line managers to compile financial reports in a certain manner. The production planning and control department, for example, has authority to require daily reports of production and material usage to be submitted on a certain form at a particular time of the day.

Control authority involves a certain amount of interpretation from the staff department. Control departments are sometimes required to interpret the organization's written procedures, and to decide what constitutes compliance with these procedures. Consequently, their "policing" authority is more than routine, and often a source of strife between line and staff. The production foreman is not likely to look kindly upon an inspection supervisor who determines that a batch of product must be turned down for not meeting quality standards. Although it would seem that such standards could be precisely set, sufficient latitude usually exists to result in the exercise of a fair degree of subjective judgment by both parties concerned.

Obviously, most of the questions regarding staff authority arise in those situations in which staff is exercising functional or control authority. Is such authority consistent with the notion that a "man should have only one boss," which is sometimes referred to as the principle of Unity of Command? Perhaps an acceptable response to this question lies in examining the source of the staff's authority. In the final analysis, staff authority is an extension of line authority. The personnel director who negotiates the labor contract has been commissioned to do this by the president of the organization. In effect, then, he is acting on behalf of the president who, in so many words, is saying, "I have delegated to the personnel director authority, my own authority, to negotiate the contract. If there are questions, they should be referred to me if they cannot be resolved through discussions with my personnel man."

The kind of authority that staff departments and personnel do *not* have should be clarified. Since the primary function of the line organization is to produce and market a product or service, the command to produce or sell is usually not issued by the staff man. Advisory departments deal with the questions of how, when, and where, but not IF a product will be manufactured.

Paradox of Line and Staff Functions

In spite of innumerable attempts to rationalize the logic of the staff's role in organization, inconsistencies persist in actuality if not in theory. It seems a paradox that staff functions are established primarily for the purpose of enabling line executives to exercise their authority more efficiently. In many instances it is apparent that the staff departments are anything but subordinate and auxiliary to the line organization. Staff groups seem quite successful in amassing a great deal of authority even beyond the types of legitimate authority discussed above. Merely accepting the explanation provided; namely, that staff authority is an extension of the authority of a higher level line manager and that staff is to act on behalf of that line executive, does little to resolve the paradox.

It is difficult to reconcile the "one boss" principle with the fact that staff managers often have the authority to command. This is true particularly in the case of control staffs. Thus, the production supervisor, even though he is accountable for results to his immediate superior in the organization chain (the plant manager), still must reckon with the demands of industrial engineers and, in labor relations matters, the personnel department. The scalar principle, if rigidly adhered to, would require that *all* commands and orders be issued through the line hierarchy. But this situation is impractical. Staff departments must have lines of communications with lower level managers.

Communications Control

Suppose, for example, a staff representative in the lower echelons of the quality control department needed to communicate with a foreman on some problem he has detected in maintaining quality standards. If strict adherence were given the scalar principle, the staff representative would have to refer the matter to his immediate supervisor, the process continuing until it was brought to the attention of the head of the staff department, who, in turn, would refer the matter to the line executive to whom he is responsible. At this point, the issue would start down the line hierarchy until it finally came to the attention of the responsible foreman. Obviously, such a situation would be extremely confusing and time-consuming. The staff representative must, as a practical matter, have lines of communications open directly to his counterpart in the line organization.

What about the question of authority? Can the staff representative and the quality control department actually command the production supervisor to do something? Theoretically, the answer is no. According to theory, the staff advisor is simply communicating to the production supervisor the meaning and interpretation of quality specifications. He can point out when requirements are not being met. He can ask for certain data and information, *since it has been established from above* in the *line organization* that this procedure will be complied with. But if the production supervisor and the staff representative disagree over interpretation or if the production supervisor were to go so far as to refuse to grant the information requested, the staff representative's only recourse, then, would be to refer the matter to *his* immediate superior. Under such circumstances of disagreement, the scalar chain principle is applied.

But does theory compare with practice? This is the perennial problem raised by those who see the paradox in line and staff authority relationships. Will the production supervisor actually express his disagreement? Theoretically, he can refuse to comply with a request of the staff man and often this does occur. However, when the production supervisor does comply, it is said that the staff representative is exercising functional authority.

Problems of Staff Versus Line Authority

The paradox alluded to above suggests many potential problems in staff-line relationships. Even a rationalization of staff's organizational role in completely logical terms leaves issues which are blurred or inconclusive. In almost every firm there is, in fact, a great deal of competition between line and staff managers; hence, the need for control. An examination of some of the sources of conflict will be of assistance to those executives who wish to understand this problem in their own organizations.

Why Staff Tends to Acquire Line Authority

Probably central to all problems of line and staff relationships is the tendency for individual staff managers to acquire and actually exercise authority far beyond theoretical limitations or intentions.

Some of the reasons are apparent simply on the basis of their place in the organization structure. Other reasons are more subtle.

Special Knowledge

The possession of special knowledge and qualifications tends to encourage the acquisition of a kind of authority. Some writers, in fact, call this the "authority of special knowledge or expertise." This kind of authority is quite understandable since many businessmen tend to defer to the specialist in their areas of knowledge. When the engineer says that a certain hardness is required in the material to withstand normal conditions, the first inclination is "he must know, after all he spent years studying to be an engineer." Likewise, employees generally are not likely to question the cost accountant's opinion that certain data are necessary for getting the true cost picture and that his procedures for compiling and reporting are sound.

It would seem that this type of authority is not necessarily undesirable. A staff man should be expected to acquire authority of this nature to some degree. Perhaps the problem involves the reluctance to weigh other factors when considering the staff specialist's recommendations. Some managers may feel uneasy about questioning any suggestion or proposal by a staff specialist, but clearly a line manager should do this. Often the line manager is in a better position to weigh all the factors and come to effective conclusions.

In some areas, the authority of special knowledge is not nearly so potent as others. This is the case particularly when the specialist deals with an area that everybody feels he knows something about. Personnel specialists, for example, are likely to experience varying degrees of "authority of special knowledge," in view of the fact that most feel knowledgeable about human relations.

More Complete Knowledge

In some cases, the staff specialist acquires authority through the simple fact that he has more information at hand, even though the information may not be specialized in nature. The production planner, for example, usually has more specialized knowledge than a production supervisor, but he has more information at hand regarding the operations of various departments. This is natural since an important function of all staff specialists is to gather facts and information about the total organization system. The very basis of staff work is that someone will specialize in an activity to which the line manager cannot give the necessary time. The mere possession of total information, then, is a factor in staff's acquiring line authority. Most people are reluctant to question the decision of those who have more information available.

Strategic Organizational Location

A staff manager often acquires line authority because he is in close contact with a high level line manager who wields a great deal of authority. A lower echelon line manager is understandably reluctant to oppose a staff officer who reports to the general manager. It takes little imagination to surmise why. The staff officer, in close contact with the high level manager, has the opportunity to get across *his* point of view. The common knowledge that a certain staff officer "has the boss' ear" is all that is needed to cause one to be wary of invoking his displeasure.

Physical Location

Regardless of the staff officer's organizational position, his mere location *physically* close to managers who have a great deal of authority is likely to result in exercising authority beyond formal specifications. The fact that somebody works "in the office" near the "chief" is enough to give pause to any other manager physically more removed. It is natural for anyone to speculate on the staff man's relationship with the top executive. If he is close physically, he must have pretty close communication with the boss. Perhaps he has lunch with the boss frequently and this provides the opportunity to make his point.

Handy "Crutch"

Some of the drift of authority toward staff can be traced to the tendency of many line managers to take the line of least resistance. In spite of what may be said, not all line managers are eager to acquire more and more authority. Many are prone to let someone else do the job. This is particularly true for those functions the line manager finds distasteful. The training and development of line managers is primarily the responsibility of the line managers themselves. Most line managers would readily agree that they have an important responsibility to carry out with regard to the development of their subordinates, yet many will leave any activity in this area to the staff specialists. To these line managers the staff stands as a ready and willing crutch upon which to rely.

Staff Man's Need for Tangible Results

To some degree, the flow of line authority to staff can be traced directly to the staff man. The results of staff work are often difficult to discern. No one knows this better than the staff man himself. Many individuals feel very uncomfortable in a situation in which they cannot see the results of their efforts. They prefer to "do it themselves" rather than counsel and recommend, with no assurance that their advice will be heeded. And even when there is evidence that their advice has been accepted and implemented, it is often difficult to connect final results with their assistance.

Some staff men are not suited temperamentally for their roles. One personal requisite is the ability to view achievements from a long-range and indirect point of view with direct, short-range results often not obvious.

Failure to Use Staff

Not all of the problems of line and staff relations concern the overextension of staff authority. Just as great a problem is the failure of line management to make maximum use of the staff assistance available to them. Often the line manager simply is not convinced that staff can help. It is a commonly held opinion that staff's viewpoint is not realistic. Their ideas are held impracticable because "they don't know what the situation really is like on the firing line." In many instances, this viewpoint represents the essence of the need for staff. The idea of the staff specialist is that he will bring into the picture a slant or an approach different from that of the line manager. Perhaps the true reason for labeling staff recommendations as "impractical" lies in the fact that staff often call for line managers to depart from present methods of doing things. There is a natural tendency to resist changing from a comfortable and familiar routine.

One practical approach of management is to initiate Compulsory Staff Advice. Before a final decision is made by the line involving matters important to the organization, staff is given the opportunity to contribute by making its recommendations. The line organization is not under obligation to accept staff's recommendations, but it is responsible for seeking and considering them honestly.

Inherent Limitations of Staff Work

Staff is overhead! It does not contribute *directly* to the company's profit. Is the added expense of staff worth it? This question must be answered by executive management. When staff values are clearcut, are their contributions worth the costs? It is not easy to evaluate staff's relative contribution in dollars and cents, and no one likes to tamper with something that looks good. Some industries can easily justify a large number of high-priced engineers. But others would have to ask themselves whether, for their purposes, a "Ford" makes more sense than a "Cadillac."

There are other limitations to staff. Staff complicates the organizational picture, often affecting the decision-making process adversely. Decision making is likely to be more prompt and clearcut when lines of authority and responsibility are simple, as in the line type organization. However, this limitation of staff is not altogether a one-sided matter. When the organizational structure is more complicated, careful planning of the staff function can improve the decision process. If the line executive can be relieved of some of the details of his function, even some involving his relationship with subordinates, such as reviewing and analyzing reports for control purposes, he is free to spend more time with his men on other matters. Nevertheless, the tendency for staff to complicate the organizational picture must be considered a limitation.

The value of staff, particularly when its prime function is to help in some phase of the planning function, is often tempered by its distance from the problem. When the staff man is remote from the "firing line" where decisions, bearing directly on the company's profit performance, are made, questions arise concerning the realism and practicality of his recommendations. Basically, this is a question of how effective a planner can be if he is not also the doer or the one who must put the plan in operation.

The value of staff also depends on the degree to which line managers use staff. Although failure to use staff departments would seem to reflect adversely on the line manager rather than the staff specialists, experience indicates that staff are often not used to their greatest potential. Assuming that the ideal utilization of staff services is not likely to be achieved, this factor must be considered a limitation of the staff function.

Curiously, the effects of staff are sometimes negative for just the opposite reason—their *overuse*. Already suggested is the tendency of some managers to rely heavily on staff to do certain things. Rather than accept the suggestions and advice of staff as an aid to their decision-making, some line managers leave the whole job to the staff. A common example is the manager who feels he can leave the training and development of subordinates to the personnel department. Not only is this procedure an abdication of a vital function, but it means that the person who can most effectively perform this function—an employee's immediate superior—takes himself out of the picture.

A final limitation of staff work lies in the nature of the function itself. Some types of staff work are difficult to perform effectively. They require personnel of very demanding qualifications. Often having authority only to propose and suggest, the staff man must be capable of persuading and motivating on a purely voluntary basis. These individuals are extremely difficult to find.

Providing Management Planning and Control Assistance

One of the prime purposes for expansion of staff use has been the realization that management planning and control can benefit greatly through the concentrated attention of specialists. Many managers still make their decisions, to a great extent, by intuition. But gradually intuitive management is being replaced by scientific methods. It has been the staff departments which have brought method and system to much of the planning and control function.

The staff specialist brings a disciplined background to management planning and control problems especially in the highly technical fields of engineering and research and the professional fields of finance, marketing, statistics, and personnel.

Not only is special knowledge brought into the planning and control processes, but the establishment of staff departments and functions assures that plans will be based on some degree of concentrated study and analysis. The general line manager who performs all functions in the management process cannot spend a great deal of time collecting, analyzing, and interpreting data. His planning would likely be based on research done in a very perfunctory manner, if at all.

Because of his training, a good staff specialist brings an analytical method to planning and controlling. He should be less prone to rely on assumptions and better able to recognize facts.

Summary

The staff function was developed primarily to assist the line organization in performing its functions. The staff man does nothing the line manager would not do himself if he had the time, special skill, and knowledge.

Staff size has multiplied in recent decades relative to the line organization. It has grown because: large organizations have posed problems of coordination and control which have exceeded the capacity of managers in the simple line organizational structure; technological and market developments have necessitated the greater use of specialized knowledge and skill; the management process itself needs to be imbued with the scientific approach.

But staff has its limitations. Predominant is cost. Staff is overhead, and its value must be weighed against its expense. There are other limitations. Staff complicates the organizational structure and relationships. The decision-making process is often delayed. The planning is separated from the doing, consequently the planners don't always see the problem firsthand. Highly qualified personnel are required. But potential values are great. In fact, hardly an organization could function in today's industrial system without use of staff. Continued employment of staff on an increasing scale is practically a certainty. The problem for management, then, is to learn to use staff. A good starting point is to understand the theoretical basis for the staff role in management. This is the first step toward bringing theory into closer harmony with practice.

CHAPTER THREE

Organization Control— Executive Action

There is growing recognition that the basic management process is similar for all managers regardless of level. An analysis of functions will show that the foreman's job and the president's job both involve basic decision problems which can be classified into the general categories of planning, organizing, motivating, and controlling. The similarity is valid only to a limited degree, however. The foreman and the president perform planning activities, but obviously there is a marked difference in the type and degree of planning. The president may be concerned with future expansion of the company's production facilities. The foreman is likely to be concerned with next week's or even tomorrow's production. The president's problem involves questions of how and where large sums of capital will be obtained for the expansion; where the facilities will be located; and who will head the new facilities. The foreman will grapple with the problems of seeing that materials are available; of checking machine loading charts; and of assignment of workers.

Both are likely to need some form of staff assistance. But the relationships that these and other managers will experience with staff managers and departments will vary. The following sections of this chapter will deal with techniques used by executives to control their staffs.

Level of Executive Action

The levels of management can be categorized as top-, middle-, and first-level supervision. This oversimplification is useful when examining the differences in control and decision-making as the management ladder is ascended.

Top Management

Top management is a relatively small group of executives who are concerned with the active and *full-time* administration of organizational affairs. (Most boards of directors would not be considered "top management" in this frame of reference.) Typically, this level of management carries such titles as president, vice president of manufacturing, vice president for sales, and, perhaps, general manager. They may be located at a headquarters office separate from operative divisions. For example, both the United States Steel Corporation and the Aluminum Company of America have their headquarters situated in large skyscrapers in downtown Pittsburgh.

A degree of physical detachment from the company's manufacturing and sales operations is indicative of the type of function top managers perform. One of the most basic differences between theirs and lower level functions involves *time*. Top management generally is not concerned with day-to-day operations. Theirs is the function of planning for the future, which may be six months or ten years away. The thinking and planning are in broad strokes of long-range programs and projects. The decisions they face are surrounded with uncertainty. Is there a market for the new product contemplated? Will a sufficient volume of sales be realized to justify a planned expansion? Shall we decentralize operations further? Or, conversely, should we be thinking in terms of centralizing in view of new electronic data processing equipment that could process information from all divisions?

Top level executives will find themselves enmeshed in problems of coordination and control on a broad scale. The vice president in charge of manufacturing, for example, will have the problem of coordinating the work of a variety of production units, some similar, others quite dissimilar. His decisions and actions will often have to ameliorate competing proposals and requests. Better coordination of his subordinate units may be possible only through greater control. This may entail limiting his subordinate's area of authority, which is undesirable if each subunit is to have as much freedom as possible in conducting its affairs.

In their roles of recommending overall company policies which will be considered by the highest organizational position or unit, these top executives will require a great deal of work in developing plans and proposing policies and programs. They know that success in getting plans, programs, and policies adopted will depend upon how effectively supportive information has been marshalled.

It is appropriate to note, at this point, that most line executives act in a staff capacity. As subordinates, themselves, their advice and recommendations are often being sought by their own superiors.

Middle Management

The line of demarcation for middle management is anything but precise. We regard them as a group of managers below the top or administrative level and above the first one or two operative levels. Typically, their titles are plant managers, superintendents, and department or divisional heads, including line and staff units.

Since the discretionary area of decision-making becomes smaller as the organizational hierarchy is descended, at least as far as major goals and policies are concerned, the middle manager will naturally concentrate his attention on different factors. He is more concerned with means rather than ends. The broad goals having been set, his function is to administer the program in the most effective manner. This is an oversimplification, of course, since the objectives established for him may be defined so broadly that he still has a great deal of policy determination to perform. The plant manager, for example, must base his overall production planning on the sales forecast. This leaves him, or his production planning unit, little to say about total production goals and product mix. But within that limitation, he does have wide latitude in organizing units, short-range scheduling, and, most important, production control.

The middle manager is likely to find himself immersed in a mixture of both long- and short-range planning and control. Particularly in the realm of facilities and manpower requirements, his view should cover a fairly long span of time. He may, for example, plan a major personnel or departmental change a year or more in advance. He won't wait until the last minute to decide who will take over a key function when the incumbent retires. Retirement of a key manager provides an opportune time to make other needed organizational changes. At the same time, many day-to-day operating problems find their way to the superintendent's and even to the plant manager's office. A dispute between engineering and production over design specifications is a typical example. Like top management, middle management must frequently cope with the problem of coordinating the various subordinate organizational units.

First Level Supervision

The first level supervisor is at the far end of the spectrum. The types of decisions he makes differ in terms both of time and of content. The production supervisor does little long-range planning and control, although ideally he probably should. But the pressures of daily problems are uppermost in his mind. He must see that daily quotas are met. A machine breakdown gets his immediate attention. Workers are absent and he must take steps to see that their functions are covered for the day. He looks over tomorrow's and next week's production schedules and checks materials and machine capacity. The office supervisor's difficulties are not basically different from that of his counterpart in production. Again, his concern is today's and tomorrow's work load. He hears complaints about clerical errors. He must make quick assignments to cover the work of absent clerks and stenographers. He is often "breaking in" a new employee.

Kinds of Staff Assistance Required by Different Level Executives

This brief description of the basic types of decisions and executive actions suggests the type of staff assistance and control needed by the various echelons. Top management will lean heavily on staff aids largely for advice and assistance in planning, especially long-range planning. Lower level managers, on the other hand, generally require the service type of staff assistance. The personnel department often performs certain functions for the first level supervisor as well as higher levels. Quality control not only advises but performs the control functions of inspection and reporting for line management. Production planning and control provides scheduling services. Basically, then, staff units and personnel at the higher levels provide assistance for the line manager to whom they are responsible, while those at the lower echelons provide assistance predominantly in the form of specialized services for the entire organization. There are exceptions, of course. A headquarters staff department may supply counsel both for the line officer from whom it is appended and their counterparts at the divisional level.

Conflicting Objectives in Executive Action

Anyone with even a limited degree of experience within an organization soon becomes aware of the endless series of conflicts among individuals and departments. Each individual has his own personal goals and these are not always consistent with those of the firm.

Conflicting objectives in executive action cannot be attributed solely to the personality factor. They are engendered by the nature of organizational objectives themselves—even the most basic ones. Offhand it would seem that the firm's basic goals can hardly be more clear: to produce a product or service desired by the customer at the appropriate level of cost and quality, supply it when and where it is needed, and thereby earn a fair profit. But translate this broad goal into the specific things that must be done and the source of conflicts immediately becomes apparent. It costs money to assure quality. How far can the firm go in this direction in the face of its cost objective? What part of earnings should be reinvested in view of the profit objective? The source of conflict in executive action starts with the firm's basic goals. The organization's overall objective has multiple elements. Furthermore, these various elements are often inconsistent with each other, as illustrated by the questions above.

The basis for conflict and disagreement is even further compounded by the nature of the organizational process. A prime reason for formal organization is to achieve specialization. We see this immediately upon the development of an organization. Below the top executive, the organization is divided into broad functional groups, such as manufacturing, sales, finance, and perhaps, engineering. *None* of these departments or segments of the organization can achieve the firm's goals *alone*. Each is responsible for some aspect of them. And each is evaluated in terms of meeting its particular goals which are, in effect, subgoals of the firm. Little imagination is needed to anticipate the obvious conflicts. Sales argues for a wider range of products and variations, pointing to the need of meeting customer demands. Manufacturing points out the possibilities of greatly reduced costs through fewer and more standardized items, and so forth.

The basis for conflict continues as the hierarchy of the organization is descended. The production supervisor concentrates on meeting schedules and keeping down costs. If operations are proceeding smoothly, he often looks unkindly upon industrial engineering's ideas for changes in methods.

One of the most disturbing sources of conflict is the nature of the line and staff relationship. Theoretically, a staff department's reason for existence is to facilitate the work of a line executive or department. Sometimes this is attempted in the form of advice and assistance in planning. Sometimes it is in the form of developing and monitoring procedures, particularly control procedures. But the prime objective of the staff department is often lost or becomes unclear, at least in the eyes of the line organization. The accounting department insists upon certain procedures and forms to be used by production managers in compiling and reporting cost data. The personnel or management development department insists upon all managers conducting periodic appraisal interviews, using the procedures and forms developed by them. Many managers may question the value of the entire procedure and particularly the appraisal form. They doubt the program's contribution to the firm's goals and begin to suspect the staff department's role in getting top management to "buy" the program.

The problem is not alleviated by the fact that it very often *is* quite difficult to determine whether or not some staff activities do contribute to the firm's goals.

The solution to the problem of conflicting objectives in executive action seems obvious. Make certain that overall goals are clearly stated. Furthermore, spell out the subgoals and plans for implementation in sufficient detail so that doubt and misinterpretation are avoided. While these efforts to integrate and coordinate the various organizational elements can never achieve perfection, considerable latitude for disagreement being possible no matter how definitively objectives may be stated, an improvement of overall executive control can be expected.

Guides for Use of Staff in Executive Control

The value of a staff unit or individual staff assistant will depend largely upon how effectively line management uses their services.

Some organizations use this factor in evaluating the performance of all managers. The principle of Compulsory Staff Advice states, in effect, that in coping with a problem or making a vital decision, the line manager should make certain staff has had a chance to make its contribution. In other words, staff is to be used and the line manager fails to meet his responsibility by not doing so.

One of the first steps in proper use of staff is developing the habit of consulting with it whenever a decision is being made in its area of competence. It is easy to overlook the staff department. Often it seems the solution is so obvious that staff's advice or service really isn't needed. But even if this were the case, the line manager should remember that failure to consult staff may undermine their morale. Like all individuals, a staff man will feel slighted if his services aren't sought. This is particularly important in the case of highly trained and specialized staff people.

There is another reason for acquiring the habit of consulting with staff. Staff people often are accused of having little insight into and appreciation of the actual "firing line" conditions. All too frequently, the charge is valid. But line managers do little to remedy the situation when they provide few opportunities for staff people to apply their skills to their problems.

Higher level managers should be sensitive to the nature of relations between their staff departments and specialists and subordinate line units. Particular care should be taken in how much freedom is allowed staff in exercising authority, even though it is "in the name" of the line manager himself. There are some things that the subordinate manager would rather hear from the "boss" himself rather than the staff assistant. The matter of status is involved. The line manager may well resent taking orders from a staff man whom he regards as lower in status. On the other hand, in many instances the staff man legitimately must have free communications lines with line managers. Some counseling on the part of the staff man's superior on how to deal with these men may avert some touchy situations.

The line manager must be sensitive to other possible pitfalls in his relations with his own staff assistants. He may find himself insulated from his subordinate line managers because he spends too much time with his staff assistants. The line manager must take great pains to make sure that all parties clearly understand the role of the staff assistants. Subordinate line managers often feel that staff exerts undue influence on his, the line manager's, own boss. He may feel insecure about staff's closeness to the boss. Under such circumstances, the subordinate line manager could become quite wary of the staff man. He may be reluctant, for example, to take a problem to the staff man even though that would be the logical source of help, for fear that the staff man would spot "weaknesses"—difficulties which might be passed on to his boss. He is loathe to have the staff man represent him in a bad light.

Whereas the line manager should develop the habit of consulting with staff in their areas of competence, he must be careful not to let this interfere with proper consultation with line subordinates. There are many instances in which the subordinate line manager is the logical source of information and advice. It is not always easy to distinguish between when it is proper to solicit the advice of one rather than the other. In fact, the distinction may not be there. It could well be that both the staff man and the line subordinate are involved in a particular problem or decision. In such case, the superior line manager might well consult with both *simultaneously*. This can avoid the appearance of talking with one about a matter involving the other or even talking "behind the back" of one. The above discussion suggests that effective use of staff does not come about automatically.

All principals involved must work at the problem diligently and consistently. The staff people themselves must recognize the possible pitfalls. Line managers do not always accept their "specialist" status in areas in which they themselves feel quite competent. Staff must constantly sell their services even when they have been granted clear and effective authority by higher management. The "acceptance" concept of authority discussed earlier is particularly appropriate. Staff may be given authority to initiate a program, but the implementation people can very effectively sabotage such programs if they do not agree with them. In many instances staff can delay moving ahead with a program sanctioned by higher management until they are certain a reasonable degree of acceptance is assured.

Staff must acquire some skill in strategy to get their ideas implemented smoothly. The authors are familiar with a large organization which planned a new and revitalized management development program that included management appraisal at all levels, continuous organizational planning, and extensive training. The staff department had the "go ahead" from top management to proceed with the entire program. The staff manager, however, wisely decided to initiate only the appraisal program. He was certain that busy line managers would rebel at embarking upon the "whole ball of wax" at the outset. Furthermore, it is better for staff itself to concentrate on one thing at a time. Executive appraisal programs are extremely difficult to implement successfully. The process of a superior evaluating his subordinate and recording it is replete with possible pitfalls. The program must be constantly studied, reanalyzed, and very probably substantially revised as it goes along. The staff department is likely to become completely engrossed in resolving the difficulties that almost inevitably arise. They themselves will want to devote full attention to just this phase of the management development program. Also, a good job in this phase of the program will help win the confidence of line management and greatly facilitate acceptance and implementation of the rest of the program.

The staff department's line superiors will play probably the key role in determining the effectiveness of staff assistance in executive action. The line executive must understand these things: the nature of the staff role; the difficulties inherent in staff's organizational situation; and the attitude of many line managers who dislike the staff man's physical and communicative proximity. The line executive must take care not to violate the line subordinate's legitimate authority.

Finally, those people served by staff must cultivate certain attitudes based upon the principle of Compulsory Staff Advice. They must understand that staff is there to help them. The authors are familiar with many line managers who say with pride that they use staff's services very infrequently. Perhaps they resent the staff's "expert" role. Often they feel that the staff man's approach is unrealistic. But the very fact that staff's slant is different ought to suggest that perhaps line management's outlook has become too permanent and somewhat intolerant. They might well consider staff's frequent allegation that line management adopts an inflexible attitude toward approaches and decisions and should take a fresh look at the situation every once in a while.

It is easy for line executives to become impervious to the difficulties that exist between staff departments and lower echelon line units. Often a top executive is completely unaware that relations are strained. In many instances they have failed to clearly spell out just what staff is to do and what its authority is to be. The feeling often is that "in time things work out and everybody gets used to the relationships that evolve naturally." Perhaps a certain type of "status quo" does evolve; but the pattern that hardens may be most un-desirable.

Provisions for Executive Development of Staff

The nature of the staff function would seem to require a very high degree of ability and qualifications on the part of staff personnel. It is surprising, then, that the particular problems of executive development of staff personnel have often been grossly neglected. A great deal of organized programming for the development of line managers is noted, but relatively little for staff, with the exception of the heads of staff organizations. Perhaps the feeling is that staff's greatest needs for development and improvement are in the areas of their specialties. Staff specialists are likely to be quite active in professional groups, such as the various engineering societies, accounting, and marketing associations. But development limited exclusively to the technical areas is shortsighted. The most knowledgeable and expert specialist cannot usually give full value to the company if he fails in the administrative process of dealing with his own subordinates and, particularly, in dealing with other managers. There is a widely known story about the farmer who resisted training in the newer methods of scientific farming because he was not farming as well as he knew how to. Likewise, the full benefit of the staff man's expertise will not be realized if he cannot facilitate its use. Usually this means being skilled in the management process.

Executive development of staff begins with selection. Everything said in these last two chapters suggests strongly that the staff man needs certain personal qualities beyond skill in his specialty. He usually must be able to get results through persuasion rather than organizational authority. Even when he does have clear authority to require adherence to his directives on the part of other managers, it is wise for him to win acceptance in advance. Clearly, then, certain individuals are "cut out" for staff work while others are not.

The staff executive role is compounded by the necessity that he wear "two hats." He exercises line authority over his own department, yet he is in a staff relationship with other departments. This suggests the need for a highly flexible type of individual.

It would seem the staff executive is placed in a rather paradoxical position. He plays two roles, each perhaps calling for a different approach. Can such an individual realistically be found? It is difficult, to be sure. But the situation can be improved by making certain that the staff executive is well grounded in management principles. If he is, he clearly understands the nature of staff and line relationships. To him, the role is not so paradoxical. He has some basis for deciding what approach is called for in the particular situation.

To illustrate the point: Management principles usually are organized within the framework of basic management functions such as planning, organizing, motivating, directing, and controlling. A production supervisor in many instances can be relatively weak in certain areas but still get along satisfactorily. Perhaps he is not much of a planner or organizer or controller in the formal sense. But he may be quite skilled in directing and motivating his subordinates. He has the knack of getting the group to work for him. A staff manager, on the other hand, will need to be skilled in all areas. He must be able to plan, organize, and control the activities of his department. At the same time, he must be skilled in directing and motivating, since he will often find it necessary to persuade other organizational elements over which he has no direct authority to undertake programs suggested by him.

One particular problem of the staff executive is keeping a firm grasp on the "whole picture" insofar as the organization is concerned. It is easy for the staff man to get deeply engrossed in his own special activity. He tends to see everything in terms of his specialty. He sees the "personnel picture" or the "finance picture." But the total organization must counterbalance the various viewpoints in order to achieve results. As mentioned earlier, staff is often accused of having an unrealistic understanding of line activities. They do not know what it is really like on "the firing line." (Of course, the same can be said about line executives in terms of seeing the specialist's point of view.) The problem for the staff executive, then, is maintaining an outlook toward the *whole* enterprise. He must be careful lest he lose sight of the firm's prime goals. He also must be careful lest he lose touch with reality as far as the rest of the organization is concerned. One solution may be job rotation. Some firms do, in fact, make it a practice to reassign staff men to line units, and vice versa, for certain periods, but this is administratively difficult. It is difficult to move a high-level executive around for a temporary period.

Some firms do not view the rotation of key executives as necessarily a temporary matter. The authors know of instances, for example, in which production executives have been moved into industrial relations positions at corporate level and vice versa. There is not necessarily any understanding that the executive is there only temporarily.

The possibilities of job rotation as a means of development for staff executives does seem limited. Another approach is to make certain that communications with other organizational elements are frequent and on a regular basis. Staff should be encouraged to consult line managers as part of their own research. Sometimes interdepartmental committees at various levels are established. While the main purpose may be to resolve a problem, such meetings can provide an avenue of communications between line and staff. The mutual understanding is helpful in promoting coordination. It is also helpful in the development of staff specialists.

In many respects, the development process for staff managers is no different from that of others. The superior-subordinate relationship is still the critical area. Like other managers, staff managers develop best when they are given increased responsibility and opportunity to make decisions. The staff executive who believes in and effectively practices delegation can do more than anyone else in helping his subordinate develop. On-the-job coaching and counseling are his opportunities for bringing the subordinate along. Encouragement and, when proper, reprimand are powerful motivational tools which only an individual's superior can exercise most effectively.

Provision for Control of Human Performance

The quantity of output in organizations is determined mainly by the performance of people rather than by the speed of machines. Consequently, great effort has been expended in the development of scientific managerial methods which facilitate the control of human performance.

Various types of work measurement techniques have been devised to assist in controlling human output. Motion and time analysis is often applied to industrial production operations. Industrial engineers establish standard times and employees are evaluated on the amount of work they produce as compared with the predetermined standards. MTM (Motion times Measurement) and work factors are two forms of time study which involve job division into standard operations, close analysis of methods, and establishment of standards for new jobs which can be defined in terms of the standard data.

Administrative work measurement is more complex than production time study because of the ordinarily subjective definition of work units. For example, it is difficult to distinguish between the typing of manuscript and the typing of statistical data, yet the latter requires much more time.

Various methods have been developed to assist in the control of administrative output. One method requires that employees record and report the type and amount of work they produce. Of course, the discerning reader will be able to detect many problems inherent in this approach.

Work sampling is a more scientific and useful control technique, since it is based upon the law of probability and sampling theory. Its purpose is to determine the relative time being spent on various productive and nonproductive activities through unbiased observation and recording of samples of work. With this method sample observations of the work of a person or group are made at random times throughout normal working hours. The larger the sample size, the more accurate will be the picture of job content and nonproductive labor.

In the aircraft and missile industries, human skills and effort are much more critical than in highly automated assembly plants or in routine office positions. The Norair Division of the Northrop Corporation has developed a model called PACE, an acronym for Performance and Cost Evaluation. PACE is a rather complicated attempt to provide management with control information about personnel requirements, budgets, scheduling, quality, and inventory shortages. This information is acquired through work sampling techniques. Analysts measure the percentage of time employees actually spend on given tasks, their idle time, and time spent away from their work area for such reasons as seeking advice from staff specialists or waiting for tools to be distributed.

The PACE measurement index represents the foundation of the system. The formula for the index is

$$\frac{A \pm B - (C + D)}{A \pm B} \times E \times 100$$

where

A = number of people assigned to a particular task
B = number of people temporarily transferred to or from the basic group
C = number of people idle as the moment of observation
D = number of people temporarily out of the work area at the moment of observation

E = group effort rating; subjective evaluation of the level of effort being exerted by the group as a whole.

The PACE measurement index involves three factors which are highly subjective: the number of people idle, the number out of the physical work area since it is often difficult to define the boundaries of a particular job, and, finally, the group effort index which requires that an observer judge the tempo of a group's effort. This third judgment is the most subjective and demands great skill on the part of the observer, who, even if highly trained, must rely on estimates of the situation. Since the PACE Index is not meaningful without a sound judgment of the group effort rating, the method has not received widespread application, as is that given to PERT (Program Evaluation and Review Technique—see Chap. Five). However, the reader may wish to delve more deeply into the problems of controlling human performance and, consequently, will desire to pursue the PACE concept in its entirety, as found in *The Quantitative Approach to Managerial Decisions.*[1]

Work measurement, in spite of the difficulty of determining a person's or group's *effort,* has many advantages. It provides current information regarding administrative and production practices and identifies areas where methods and scheduling might be improved. Work measurement data can be used to determine estimates of labor costs, and can be used to control the input of company training programs.

Control of Managerial Quality

Management Audit

The quality of management is probably the single most important factor determining the future success or failure of an organization. The economy may take a turn for the worse, competition may become excessive, or the consumer may change his buying habits, but sound management will be able to adapt to such adverse conditions. Why, then, does business concentrate so heavily on the accuracy of its accounting reports in measuring the quality or effectiveness of organizational performance? Perhaps tradition or government regulation has forced this type of control, but it appears that

---

[1] L. W. Hein. Englewood Cliffs, New Jersey: Prentice-Hall, Inc., 1967, pp. 261–284.

management often *assumes* that the organization is and will remain in good condition if a group of public examiners approves the financial records. Actually, this assumption is dangerous since many symptoms of impending trouble never appear in the accounting statements. Failure to establish short- and long-range objectives, increasing labor turnover, poor quality, lack of market research, and ineffective maintenance are all signs of organizational decay, but not identifiable in financial records.

If management were subjected to the same type of audit as are the organization's finances, much greater benefits would accrue. Managerial effectiveness or ineffectiveness pervades the entire organization and, consequently, improvement in the performance of management as a whole will be reflected in each of the functional areas, including that of finance.

Various methods are available by which an organization can evaluate its managerial performance. One approach which has met with a degree of success is the internal management audit developed by Jackson Martindell.[2] Management examines itself by completing an extensive questionnaire based on Martindell's "principles of management." This control technique has some shortcomings because organizations are diverse in their objectives and functions. Therefore, a standard questionnaire will probably not be appropriate for all organizations. In addition, a lack of agreement on terminology and self-evaluation limits reliable conclusions. A reasonable alternative to the internal audit is an independent appraisal performed by a qualified consulting agency. This approach permits evaluation of overall managerial effectiveness by persons skilled in the application of analytic techniques.

Performance Appraisal

The purpose of managerial appraisal is to measure and evaluate the current and potential performance of individuals. Various methods have been used to gather information about performance. These include supervisory completed graphic rating scales, management assessment centers, peer group ratings, inbox-outbox decision-making tests, group appraisals, critical incidents, and business games.

No organization has been able to discover a completely satis-

---

[2] Jackson Martindell, *Manual of Excellent Managements.* New York: American Institute of Management, 1957.

factory method for evaluating its managerial personnel. Each technique has certain advantages and disadvantages. However, most organizations agree that some attempt must be made to evaluate performance in order to provide information for the control of the overall system, as well as of promotion, salary, transfer, recruiting, training, and placement decisions. In addition, there are indirect motivational advantages associated with well-controlled and fairly administered appraisal programs, since individuals realize that their work is evaluated and that, when promotion decisions are made, their qualifications will not be inadvertently overlooked.

Results of a recent study by the consulting firm of Booz, Allen, and Hamilton indicated that approximately 35 percent of the nation's executives are promotable to higher level positions, that 50 percent are well qualified for their present positions, and that 15 percent should be transferred or released because of incompetence. These statistics indicate that some caution should be exercised when attempting to build quality into upper management. Organizations should attempt to assure that their most qualified supervisory personnel are promoted to upper levels. This strategy will help to prevent the loss of good people as well as to provide optimum decision-making capabilities at top management levels.

When developing an appraisal program, it is generally necessary to adopt the following procedures:

Establish objectives of program. Remember that most managers resist playing the role of "judge" when they also have to serve as counselors. Consequently, it is unwise to plan a program which is to serve for both performance evaluation and guidance or individual development purposes. If the person making the rating is asked to discuss a subordinate's weaknesses with him, it is likely that the superior will be overly lenient and, therefore, distort the information relayed to higher management. Progressive companies, realizing the value of each of these objectives, establish one program for appraisal and feedback on performance and a second for counseling and review sessions.

Determine who will perform ratings. Usually a person's immediate superior performs the initial rating with subsequent endorsement by the next higher level manager. This procedure may help to control the amount of bias and personal subjectivity in certain cases, but unless the endorser is thoroughly familiar with the job performance of the ratee, he may destroy the validity of the rating. It is recommended that the immediate superior perform the rating since he ordinarily has the best information about the subordinate to be rated.

Establish rating interval. Annual appraisal is common. More frequent evaluations are costly and often weaken the effectiveness of the system. An employee probably should not be rated until he has been on a particular job for at least a year. Special situations will arise, however, when the subject should be evaluated out of the normal pattern. For instance, his supervisor is transferred or he himself leaves the organization.

Determine criteria for evaluation. This is probably the most difficult task in developing a performance control model. Many appraisal systems in current use rely on such global traits as dependability, initiative, judgment, attitude, leadership, and acceptance. Granted, these are quite important for most managers to have. In fact, it would be fine if all personnel possessed them. But there is no way to measure them effectively and, if it were possible to measure them, no one is certain that they are all the traits necessary for the best managers. Evaluators have different concepts of these global traits and the degree to which each of their subordinates possesses them. Consequently, it is difficult to control the "halo" effect in which a man rated high on one trait is automatically high on the others and vice versa.

What is desired is a set of dimensions which measure a person's job performance rather than what one person "thinks" about another. Performance criteria should represent a person's overall contribution to the organization and should be observable, discriminatory, and universally applicable. The following list provides an example of criteria which should be considered when evaluating managerial performance. The items reflect an approach which emphasizes planning, organizing, controlling, and decision-making capabilities as well as the personal traits usually associated with effective leadership. The following phrases describe what is normally classed as good management. Admittedly, no scientific analysis has been accomplished which proves the assumption but it would be difficult to find fault with a manager who fits this model.

An effective and efficient manager usually

Establishes definite long-run goals for his organizational unit which are consistent with the goals of the total system.

Establishes short-range goals for his organizational unit.

Provides incentives for improvement of job performance.

Organizes the work of his unit and plans the distribution of the work.

Establishes priorities and takes action on the basis of the importance of the problem.

Establishes flexible standards and uses these standards to manage by the exception principle.

Gathers information before making important decisions when time is available.

Establishes procedures to aid in the making of routine decisions.

Uses a systematic approach to problem solving.

Views problems from the vantage point of the total organization rather than from the narrow viewpoint of his own unit.

Considers alternatives before making final decisions.

Permits subordinates to participate in decisions which affect them when appropriate.

Provides formal orientation for new employees.

Holds regular meetings with subordinates.

Communicates with subordinates, superiors, and peers.

Molds cohesive work units whose goals are consistent with those of the total system.

Accomplishes a large amount of work which is of good quality.

Is courteous to superiors, peers, and subordinates.

Respects the ideas of others.

Develops subordinates through training and personal advice.

Exhibits tact in his dealings with others.

Speaks clearly and concisely before groups.

Is in good health, mental and physical.

Dresses well to suit the occasion.

Is seldom late for work.

Offers creative and logical suggestions for improving his operations.

Observes procedures and regulations on most occasions.

Follows directions of higher level managers on most occasions.

Is resourceful when confronted with unique situations.

Shows genuine enthusiasm toward his work and in his personal relations with others.

Appears to know the capabilities and limitations of his subordinates.

Has a full understanding of his own authority and responsibility.

Is willing to try new methods.

Has the confidence of his subordinates.

Commands respect through his intelligence, appearance, and personality.

Select a method for collecting evaluation data. Rating forms are quick, simple, and probably the most objective way of relaying data from the mind of the supervisor to those persons who will ultimately use the information. Graphic rating scales which allow for about five degrees of classification are in common use. They usually have at the extremes "superior" and "very poor" with "average" used in the middle. It has been found that the tendency is to rate most personnel somewhere between "satisfactory" and "good"; consequently, the information which is conveyed is not very discriminatory. Some firms have been changing to a "forced choice" technique where the rater is asked to select from a group of four descriptive items (two favorable and two unfavorable) the item which best describes the subject and the one least like him. Weighting methods are then applied, and the results of this technique have been better than the typical graphic rating scale. It is beyond the scope of this text to explain the statistical tests which can be applied to the development of valid forced choice rating forms, but if the reader wishes to pursue the matter, he should refer to any basic statistics book under the heading of nonparametric statistics, especially the Chi-Square Method.

Summary

The purpose of organizational structure and procedures and the function of staff are to facilitate executive control. Staff should provide expert knowledge, perform functions requiring special attention, and enable top management to achieve its goals. But often in the process of facilitating executive control, some of the bitterest rivalries and conflicts evolve from the line-staff relationship.

Effective use of staff is not an automatic thing. All elements of the organization must understand staff's role, including staff personnel themselves. But the key, more often than not, to effective use of staff lies with staff's line superiors. They must be aware of the nature of relationships inherent between their line and staff subordinates. It is easy to assume that all is progressing smoothly, unaware of the "hidden agendas" that exist between line and staff subordinates. The line executive must reflect on the implications of how he uses his staff subordinates.

Staff must be careful in how it attempts to get programs started. That it should take initiative in getting a program implemented seems indisputable. Staff should constantly be on the lookout for ways and means of improvements. They should not wait for the impetus to come from other organizational units. But it should be careful in how it approaches a new proposal. Often it is wise to win approval in advance on a voluntary basis.

The measurement and control of staff work has lagged behind that of line work. But, with staff costs increasing tremendously, top management is giving this area more attention. The difficulty in establishing standards for the control of staff work is rooted in the singular nature of many of its activities. It is also a result of the difficulty of measuring directly the impact of staff's activities in terms of the organization's prime goals. But work sampling and systems analysis do provide some indirect approaches.

In view of the staff's role in the organization, it is imperative that the selection and development of staff managers proceed with greater care. The staff manager requires certain personal qualities, especially when his role is largely advisory in nature. At the same time, staff executives exercise line authority within their own department. Such diversity strongly underlines the necessity for staff executives to be well grounded in management principles and the administrative processes.

Managerial Control through Financial Statements and Accounting Analyses

Introduction

Businesses acquire goods and services, transform them into something different, and dispose of them in their new form. The accounts of a business form a record of the flow of these goods and services. All goods and services are acquired in the necessary quantity and at the lowest price consistent with a given quality. Goods and services are disposed of by a business similarly with the basic factors essentially reversed. Thus, the accounting record presents an historical chronology of the events of a business.

Control

One task of management is to *control* the future transactions and transformations of the business. Control is used here to mean optimization, that is, the condition most conducive to the goals of the business. Control does not necessarily denote a minimum, but merely an outcome desired by management. Controls are absolutely necessary in order to manage a business. Without control, the future course of events of a business will vary at random and the business will become unmanageable.

In order to proceed in an orderly fashion, overall control of a business will be discussed under the following areas:

1. Liquidity Control
2. General Financial Condition Control
3. Profitability Control

Liquidity refers to the ability of a business to meet its current debts as they mature. Financial condition refers to the long-term balance between debt and owners' equity. Profitability refers to the ability of a company to earn a profit over a continuing period of time. This last area of control is of ultimate importance to management because profit is the prime requisite to continuation of the business and it will be discussed in greater detail than the other two areas.

Accounting Concepts for Control

Accounting is the language of a business and it is necessary to have knowledge of accounting concepts and terminology in order to be able to read financial statements. Accounting treats a business as an entity in its own right separate and apart from its owners or managers. This entity engages in transactions in the open market with other firms and individuals. These transactions form the accounting record. Although accountants are sometimes criticized for it, they continue to record a firm's transactions at the actual price experienced in the marketplace. Opponents contend that the exchange price of an item purchased many years ago may no longer be realistic. The results of a firm's transactions are presented in periodic financial statements, which ordinarily consist of a balance sheet, an income statement, and sometimes a statement of sources and applications of funds or a statement of cash flow.

Balance Sheet

The balance sheet of Specialty Products Company as of December 31, 1966, appears in Exhibit A on the following page. It portrays the financial position of the company as of a given instant in time; in this case, as of the close of business on December 31, 1966. The balance sheet shows assets of the business and the sources of

SPECIALTY PRODUCTS COMPANY

CONSOLIDATED BALANCE SHEET
As of December 31, 1966

Exhibit A

Assets

Current Assets				
Cash			$ 31,000	4.43%
Marketable Securities			$ 10,000	1.43
Accounts Receivable		$ 99,000		
Less Reserve for Bad Debts		3,000	96,000	13.71
Inventories*			80,000	11.43
Prepaid Expenses			4,000	0.57
Total			$221,000	31.57%
Investments				
Investment in Affiliated Companies				
(not consolidated)		$ 40,000		5.72%
Other Investments†		30,000		4.29
Bond Sinking Fund		20,000		2.86
Total			90,000	12.87%
Fixed Assets				
Land		$ 30,000		4.29%
Plant and Equipment	$350,000			
Less: Accumulated				
Depreciation	80,000	270,000		38.56
Total			300,000	42.85%
Other Assets				
Deferred Charges		$ 19,000		2.71%
Patents and Goodwill		70,000		10.00
Total			89,000	12.71%
			$700,000	100.00%

those assets. Assets comprise all goods, services, money, and credit that have been received by the company and remain unused on the date of the balance sheet. They are classified as follows:

Current. Cash and other assets which will be converted into cash within the normal operating cycle of the business or one year whichever is longer.

Investments. Assets held for the purpose of exercising control over other enterprises or for long term investment.

Fixed Assets. Noncurrent tangible assets used in the operation of the business (plant, equipment, buildings, and similar items).

Other Assets. Intangible fixed assets (patents and goodwill) and others which do not fall under the three prior classifications. Intangible fixed assets are sometimes shown under a separate heading and occasionally with the tangible fixed assets.

CONSOLIDATED BALANCE SHEET (Continued)

Liabilities and Owners' Equity

Current Liabilities				
Accounts Payable			$ 18,000	2.56%
Notes Papable			40,000	5.72
Accrued Taxes, Wages and				
Other Expenses			35,000	5.00
Total			$ 93,000	13.28%
Long-Term Liabilities				
6% Mortgage Bonds Payable			100,000	14.29
Total Liabilities			$193,000	27.57%
Owners' Equity				
6% Preferred Stock par $10				
5,000 shares issued and				
outstanding	$ 50,000			7.14%
Common Stock no par				
10,000 shares issued and				
outstanding	250,000			35.72
Capital Paid in Excess				
of par	50,000			7.14
Total Invested Capital		$350,000		50.00
Retained Earnings Appropriated				
for Contingencies	50,000			7.14%
Retained Earnings Appropriated				
for Bond Retirement	20,000			2.86
Retained Earnings—Free	87,000			12.43
Total Earned Capital		157,000		22.43%
Total Owners' Equity			507,000	72.43
			$700,000	100.00%

* Valued on last-in, first-out basis
† Valued at cost or market, whichever is lower

Sources of assets generally represent promises of the entity (in this case Specialty Products Company) to the various persons who provided the assets which the company will be able to use in the future. These sources are reported in two classifications: Liabilities (promises to creditors) and Owners' Equity (promises to owners). Liabilities are further classified as follows:

Current. Those which can reasonably be expected to be paid from current assets.
Long Term. Those which will not be paid within a year of the date of the balance sheet.

Owners' Equity is further classified as follows:

Preferred Stock. Stock which has preferential rights to dividends and/or assets upon dissolution. The maximum dividend on preferred stock is normally fixed, and preferred stock normally does not have any voting privileges. There may be more than one kind.

Common Stock. Stock to which no preferences over any other class of stock are granted. It is the stock with the greatest risk and the potential for the greatest gain. It usually carries the voting privilege.

Capital Paid in Excess of Par. Amounts in excess of par or stated value contributed by stockholders over and above the amounts in the Preferred and Common stock categories.

Retained Earnings. Net earnings of the company from its founding or other specified date which have not been paid out in dividends. Often a portion of this amount is restricted, that is, it will not be paid to the stockholders in dividends in the near future. The remainder is termed "free" Retained Earnings and this is the amount that *could* be paid now in dividends if the company has the cash necessary to do so.

Balance Sheet Notes

Often there are footnotes to the balance sheet which explain some of the items appearing therein. These notes also explain executory contracts such as leases to which the company is a party. These notes should always be read carefully in order to determine the basis of the figures reported in the body of the balance sheet and to learn of contracts not reflected directly in the balance sheet.

Income Statement

The income statement of Specialty Products Company for the fiscal year ended December 31, 1966, appears below.

Attached to the bottom of this particular statement is a reconciliation of the beginning and ending balances of retained earnings. This statement is divided into the following sections:

Revenues. Dollar value of goods and services provided customers less returns and allowances of these items.

Cost of Goods Sold. The purchased or manufactured cost to Specialty Products Company of the goods sold during the year.

Expenses. All other operating expenses necessary to operate the business during 1966.

Other Income and Expense. Other items of income and expense not directly related to the production and sale of the primary product or service of the company.

Retained Earnings Reconciliation. Items that increased or decreased re-

SPECIALTY PRODUCTS COMPANY

STATEMENT OF INCOME
For the Year Ended December 31, 1966

		Exhibit B
Gross Sales	$970,000	
Sales Returns and Allowances	20,000	
Net Sales		$950,000
Cost of Goods Sold		685,000
Gross Profit on Sales		$265,000
Expenses		
Selling	$146,000	
Administrative	71,000	
Total		217,000
Net Income from Operations		$ 48,000
Other Income & Expense		
Interest Expense—Notes	$ 900	
Interest Expense—Bonds	$ 6,000	
Interest Income	(500)	
Total, Net		6,400
Net Income before Federal Income Tax		$ 41,600
Federal Income Tax		15,600
Net Income		$ 26,000
Retained Earnings, January 1, 1966		174,000
Total		$200,000
Deduct		
Dividends—Preferred Stock	$ 3,000	
Dividends—Common Stock	20,000	
Flood Loss	20,000	
Total		43,000
Retained Earnings, December 31, 1966		$157,000

tained earnings during the year that were not reported in the income statement proper. Some of these items were excluded from the determination of net income because they represented distributions of income (dividends) and others were excluded because they were considered extraordinary and nonrecurring and it was felt by management that inclusion in the determination would have been misleading (for example, flood loss). The reconciliation of retained earnings is something reported in a separate statement.

Income Statement Notes

Income statement notes often explain the method used for determining the valuation of cost of goods sold and inventory, the method used to depreciate long-lived assets, and some explanation of any extraordinary gains and losses included either in the determination of income or taken directly to retained earnings.

Other Financial Statements

It is becoming more common for companies to report in statement form other data than are included in the two basic statements. Exhibit C, which is shown below, presents a statement of cash flow of Specialty Products Company for the year 1966. This statement, as the name implies, merely shows the sources and uses of cash during the year. It should be emphasized that this statement bears no necessary relationship to the income statement. They report entirely different things.

Another statement that is often seen today is a statement of sources and applications of funds. Such a statement for 1966 of the Specialty Products Company is shown in Exhibit D. This statement is similar to the statement of cash flow except that its scope is broadened somewhat. "Funds" are defined by accountants to be the net

SPECIALTY PRODUCTS COMPANY

STATEMENT OF CASH FLOW
For the Year 1966

Exhibit C

Cash Provided by:		
Operations		
Net Income for Period		$ 26,000
Charges to Income not Affecting Cash:		
Depreciation of Plant and Equipment	$15,000	
Amortization of Deferred Charges	1,000	16,000
Total Provided by Operations		$ 42,000
Reduction of Accounts Receivable		24,000
Reduction of Prepaid Expenses		1,000
Sale of Marketable Securities		10,000
Sale of Investments		9,000
Total Cash Provided		$ 86,000
Cash Applied to:		
Purchase of Equipment	$10,000	
Increase Bond Sinking Fund	4,000	
Repair Flood Damage	20,000	
Increase Inventories	10,000	
Reduce Accounts Payable	22,000	
Reduce Notes Payable	1,000	
Reduce Accruals Payable	10,000	
Payment of Dividends	23,000	
Total Cash Applied		100,000
Reduction in Cash Balance		$ 14,000
Cash Balance January 1, 1966		45,000
Cash Balance December 31, 1966		$ 31,000

sum of current assets less current liabilities. Therefore, this statement depicts the change during a period of time in this net sum. It should be pointed out that ordinarily a company reports either cash flow or funds flow but rarely both. The funds statement includes, in addition to cash, other assets which are readily converted to cash and liabilities which will soon have to be paid with cash. In effect, then, the funds statement is a cash flow statement which includes anticipated cash flows as well as those which in fact occurred.

Accounting Statements Summarized

Basic accounting data and reports have been briefly presented. In the form in which the statements have been presented they represent historical reports of accomplishment and financial position. There are certain relationships among the various components of the statements which can be computed in order to learn more about the prosperity of a business. However, much more can be learned from detailed analysis of several sets of statements covering several years of a company's life. A series of analysis techniques will be presented next in order to develop the concept of control through use of financial statements.

SPECIALTY PRODUCTS COMPANY

STATEMENT OF SOURCES AND APPLICATIONS OF FUNDS
For the Year 1966

Exhibit D

Funds Provided by		
Operations		
Net Income for Period	$26,000	
Charges to Income not Affecting Working Capital		
Depreciation of Plant and Equipment	15,000	
Amortization of Deferred Charges	1,000	$ 42,000
Sale of Investments		9,000
Total Provided		$ 51,000
Funds Applied to		
Purchase of Equipment	$10,000	
Increase Bond Sinking Fund	4,000	
Payment of Dividends	23,000	
Repair Flood Damage	20,000	
Total Applied		57,000
Decrease in Working Capital		$ (6,000)
Net Working Capital, January 1, 1966		134,000
Net Working Capital, December 31, 1966		$128,000

Vertical Analysis

Vertical analysis expresses in percentages the figures on the financial statements of a given year. This tends to give a better idea of relative size of the various components of financial position or income than statements that report only the aggregate amount of cash, accounts payable, operating expenses, and so on. Often these aggregate

SPECIALTY PRODUCTS COMPANY

COMPARATIVE BALANCE SHEETS
December 31, 1966 and 1965
($000 omitted)

Exhibit E

	Amount		Percent of Total		Increase Decrease*	Ratio 1966 to 1965
	1966	1965	1966	1965		
Current Assets						
Cash	$ 31	$ 45	4.43	6.00	$14*	0.69
Marketable Securities	10	20	1.43	2.67	10*	0.50
Accounts Receivable, Net	96	120	13.71	16.00	24*	0.80
Inventories	80	70	11.43	9.33	10	1.14
Prepaid Expenses	4	5	0.57	0.67	1*	0.80
Total Current Assets	$221	$260	31.57	34.67	$39*	0.85
Investments						
Investments—Affiliated Companies	$ 40	$ 40	5.72	5.33	$—	1.00
Other Investments	30	39	4.29	5.20	9*	0.77
Bond Sinking Fund	20	16	2.86	2.13	4	1.25
Total Investments	$ 90	$ 95	12.87	12.66	$ 5*	0.95
Fixed Assets						
Land	$ 30	$ 30	4.29	4.00	$—	1.00
Plant and Equipment, Net of Depreciation	270	275	38.56	36.67	5*	0.98
Total Fixed Assets	$300	$305	42.85	40.67	$ 5*	0.98
Other Assets						
Deferred Charges	$ 19	$ 20	2.71	2.67	$ 1*	0.95
Patents and Goodwill	70	70	10.00	9.33	—	1.00
Total Other Assets	$ 89	$ 90	12.71	12.00	$ 1*	0.99
Total Assets	$700	$750	100.00	100.00	$50*	0.93

amounts are quite large for even a company of moderate size and the relationships, therefore, become obscured. In order to illustrate the benefit that can be derived from vertical analysis, a complete set of financial statements and supporting schedules for Specialty Products Company appears in Exhibits E through H. These statements present a comparative view of the most current two years' operations and financial position. By reference to the columns of the statements

COMPARATIVE BALANCE SHEETS (Continued)

	Amount		Percent of Total		Increase Decrease*	Ratio 1966 to 1965
	1966	1965	1966	1965		
Current Liabilities						
Accounts Payable	$ 18	$ 40	2.57	5.33	$22*	0.45
Notes Payable	40	41	5.71	5.47	1*	0.98
Accrued Taxes, Wages, and Other Accrued Items	35	45	5.00	6.00	10*	0.78
Total Current Liabilities	$ 93	$126	13.28	16.80	$33*	0.74
Long Term Liabilities						
6% Bonds Payable	$100	$100	14.29	13.33	$—	1.00
Owners' Equity						
Invested Capital						
Preferred Stock	$ 50	$ 50	7.14	6.67	$—	1.00
Common Stock	250	250	35.72	33.33	—	1.00
Capital Paid in Excess of Par	50	50	7.14	6.67	—	1.00
Total Invested Capital	$350	$350	50.00	46.67		1.00
Earned Capital						
Retained Earnings Appropriated for Contingencies	$ 50		7.14		$50	
Retained Earnings Appropriated for Bond Retirement	20	$ 16	2.86	2.13	4	1.25
Free Retained Earnings	87	158	12.43	21.07	71*	0.55
Total Earned Capital	$157	$174	22.43	23.20	$17*	0.90
Total Owners' Equity	$507	$524	72.43	69.87	$17*	0.97
Total Liabilities and Owners' Equity	$700	$750	100.00	100.00	$50*	0.93

SPECIALTY PRODUCTS COMPANY

COMPARATIVE CONSOLIDATED STATEMENT OF INCOME
For the Years Ended December 31, 1966 and 1965

Exhibit F

	Amount		Percent of Net Sales		Increase Decrease*	Ratio 1966 to 1965
	1966	1965	1966	1965		
Gross Sales	$970,000	$787,000	102.11	103.55	$183,000	1.23
Sales Returns and Allowances	20,000	27,000	2.11	3.55	7,000*	0.74
Net Sales	$950,000	$760,000	100.00	100.00	$190,000	1.25
Cost of Goods Sold—Exhibit G	685,000	583,000	72.11	76.71	102,000	1.17
Gross Profit on Sales	$265,000	$177,000	27.89	23.29	$ 88,000	1.50
Expenses—Exihibit H						
Selling	$146,000	$ 89,000	15.37	11.71	$ 57,000	1.64
Administrative	71,000	47,000	7.47	6.18	24,000	1.51
Total	$217,000	$136,000	22.84	17.89	$ 81,000	1.60
Net Income from Operations	$ 48,000	$ 41,000	5.05	5.40	$ 7,000	1.17
Other Income and Expense Interest Expenses						
On Notes Payable	$ 900	$ 700				
On Bonds Payable	6,000	6,000				
Total	$ 6,900	$ 6,700				
Interest Income on Securities	500	400				
Net Financial Expense	$ 6,400	$ 6,300	0.67	0.83	100	1.02
Net Income before Federal Income Tax	$ 41,600	$ 34,700	4.38	4.57	$ 6,900	1.20
Federal Income Tax	15,600	12,700	1.64	1.67	2,900	1.23
Net Income	$ 26,000	$ 22,000	2.74	2.90	$ 4,000	1.18

titled "Percent of Total," the percentage breakdown of the various operating and position components can be observed. By reference to Exhibit E, for example, it can be seen that accounts payable constituted 5.33 percent of total liabilities and owners' equity in 1965. To take another example, by reference to Exhibit F, it can be seen that selling expenses amounted to 15.37 percent of net sales in 1966. By further reference to Exhibit H, a more detailed presentation of the items making up this 15.37 percent can be found. For example, advertising amounted to 8.42 percent of the 15.37 percent or roughly 55

SPECIALTY PRODUCTS COMPANY

COMPARATIVE STATEMENT OF COST OF GOODS MANUFACTURED AND SOLD
For the Years Ended December 31, 1966 and 1965

Exhibit G

	Amount		Percent of Cost of Manufacturing		Increase Decrease*	Ratio 1966 to 1965
	1966	1965	1966	1965		
Cost of Goods Manufactured						
Raw Materials						
Inventory—Beginning of Year	$ 23,000	$ 21,000			$ 2,000	
Purchases	237,000	215,000			22,000	
Total	$260,000	$236,000			$ 24,000	
Inventory—End of Year	26,000	23,000			3,000	
Materials Used	$234,000	$213,000	33.82	36.29	$ 21,000	1.10
Direct Labor	316,000	253,000	45.66	43.10	63,000	1.25
Manufacturing Expenses	142,000	121,000	20.52	20.61	21,000	1.07
Cost of Manufacturing	$692,000	$587,000	100.00	100.00	$105,000	1.17
Goods in Process Inventory Beginning of Year	14,000	13,000				
Total	$706,000	$600,000				
Goods in Process Inventory End of Year	16,000	14,000				
Cost of Goods Manufactured	$690,000	$586,000			$104,000	1.18
Finished Goods—Beginning of Year	33,000	30,000				
Total	$723,000	$616,000				
Finished Goods—End of Year	38,000	33,000				
Cost of Goods Sold	$685,000	$583,000			$102,000	1.18

percent of it. In general, vertical analysis aids in bringing to the fore the relative amounts of the components of assets, equities, income, and expense.

Horizontal Analysis

Vertical analysis is very helpful in observing the relative amounts of the components of financial statements but it does not give any information concerning trends or intercompany comparisons. In order

SPECIALTY PRODUCTS COMPANY

COMPARATIVE SCHEDULE OF SELLING AND ADMINISTRATIVE EXPENSES
For Years Ended December 31, 1966 and 1965

Exhibit H

	Amount		Percent of Net Sales		Increase Decrease*	Ratio 1966 to 1965
	1966	1965	1966	1965		
Selling expenses						
Salesmen's Salaries and Payroll Taxes	$ 29,000	$17,000	3.06	2.24	$12,000	1.71
Salesmen's Traveling Expenses	27,000	18,000	2.84	2.37	9,000	1.50
Advertising	80,000	45,000	8.42	5.92	35,000	1.78
Freight Out	8,000	6,000	0.84	0.79	2,000	1.33
Miscellaneous	2,000	3,000	0.21	0.39	1,000*	0.67
Total	$146,000	$89,000	15.37	11.71	$57,000	1.64
Administrative expenses						
Officers' Salaries and Payroll Taxes	$ 24,000	$13,000	2.52	1.71	$11,000	1.85
Office Salaries and Payroll Taxes	26,000	20,000	2.74	2.64	6,000	1.30
Stationery and Supplies	3,000	2,000	0.32	0.26	1,000	1.50
Postage, Telephone, and Telegraph	3,000	2,000	0.32	0.26	1,000	1.50
Depreciation of Furniture and Fixtures	1,000	1,000	0.10	0.13	—	1.00
Bad Debts Expense	13,000	7,000	1.37	0.92	6,000	1.86
Miscellaneous	1,000	2,000	0.10	0.26	1,000*	0.50
Total	$ 71,000	$47,000	7.47	6.18	$24,000	1.51

to derive this information, horizontal analysis is necessary. This type of analysis consists of placing the figures for two or more years for one company or the same year for two or more companies in one statement. Percentages should be included to facilitate comparisons. Having done this, a basis of comparison is afforded which is important for an appreciation of trends and significance of the various figures. Exhibits E through H contain comparative figures for the last two years of operations of Specialty Products Company. Using the figures for two years, the information derived from vertical analysis can be expanded. By vertical analysis it was learned that accounts payable constituted 5.33 percent of total equities at December 31, 1965. Referring again to Exhibit E, it can be seen by using horizontal analysis that accounts payable totaled 2.57 percent of total equities one year later at December 31, 1966, or only 0.45 times as much. There has been, in effect, a significant decrease in the relative amount of accounts payable, a healthy trend normally. Taking another example, it was observed using vertical analysis that selling expenses amounted to 15.37 percent of net sales in 1966. Exhibit F also shows that this same item totaled 11.71 percent in 1965, an increase of 64 percent from 1965 to 1966. This represents a very substantial increase in an expense item and, in order to control it in the future, a manager would want to analyze it further to determine the specific selling expense items that caused the increase. This further information is included in Exhibit H, which indicates that all components of selling expense increased with the exception of miscellaneous selling expense. The selling expenses exhibiting the most rapid increases can be pinpointed. For example, advertising increased the most at 78 percent. This expense is one which is completely controllable and is usually determined completely by management policy. Having observed this big increase in amount through the use of horizontal analysis, the managers of Specialty Products Company may now wish to revise future policy with respect to advertising.

Summary of Vertical and Horizontal Analysis

As stated previously, management must control three basic aspects of a company's operations: profitability, liquidity (current debt payment), and general financial condition (debt-equity balance). Trends and comparisons of the various components of all of these important aspects of the operation of a business can be derived with the use of vertical and horizontal analysis. The examples given were necessarily brief. One example of the use of these types of analyses was given for a liquidity item (accounts payable) and one for a profitability item (selling expense). The reader may further analyze the progress of Specialty Products Company through the use of these types of analyses as the information given is complete.

Ratio Analysis

In the preceding discussion of statement analysis, figures appearing in financial statements were analyzed and compared with figures appearing in the same sections of the statements. Sometimes there are figures in different parts of the same statement or in completely different statements that should normally bear a close relationship. Ratio analysis is used to derive information about these closely related items scattered throughout the entire set of financial statements. Ratio analysis might be used to determine trends within the same company or to determine comparisons between two different companies in the same industry. Some of the more useful ratios are computed below grouped into profitability ratios, liquidity ratios, and general financial condition ratios. To illustrate each, ratios have been computed for Specialty Products Company for 1966.

Profitability Ratios

Number of Times Bond Interest Earned

$$\frac{\text{Net Income before Taxes and Bond Interest}}{\text{Bond Interest}}$$

$$= \frac{\$41,600 + \$6,000}{\$6,000} = 7.9 \text{ times}$$

The higher the ratio the more likely that the bond interest can be paid.

Number of Times Preferred Dividends Earned

$$\frac{\text{Net Income after Taxes}}{\text{Preferred Dividends}} = \frac{\$26,000}{\$3,000} = 8.7 \text{ times}$$

The higher the ratio the more likely that it will be possible for the company to pay the preferred dividends.

Return on Common Stockholders' Investment

$$\frac{\text{Net Income after Taxes minus Preferred Dividends}}{\text{Average Common Stockholders' Investment}}$$

$$= \frac{\$26,000 - \$3,000}{\$465,500} = 4.9 \text{ percent}$$

Average Common Stockholders' Investment

$$= \left\{ \begin{array}{l} \text{Beginning + Ending Balances of Common} \\ \text{Stock, Capital Surplus, and Earned} \\ \text{Surplus} \div 2 \end{array} \right\}$$

$$= \frac{\$250,000 + \$250,000}{2} + \frac{\$50,000 + \$50,000}{2}$$

$$+ \frac{\$174,000 + \$157,000}{2} = \$465,500$$

Earnings per Share of Common Stock

$$\frac{\text{Net Income after Taxes}}{\text{Number of Shares of Common Outstanding}} = \frac{\$26,000}{10,000} = \$2.60 \text{ a share}$$

Book Value per Share of Common Stock

$$\frac{\text{Common Stock} + \text{Capital Surplus} + \text{Earned Surplus}}{\text{Number of Shares of Common Stock Outstanding}}$$

$$= \frac{\$250,000 + \$50,000 + \$157,000}{10,000} = \$45.70 \text{ a share}$$

Liquidity Ratios

Current Ratio—measures ability to pay current liabilities.

$$\frac{\text{Current Assets}}{\text{Current Liabilities}} = \frac{\$221,000}{\$93,000} = 2.4 \text{ to } 1$$

The higher the ratio the safer the financial position of the company and the less the chance of insolvency. However, too high a ratio is an indication of too much capital tied up in current assets which could be better used for other purposes. A ratio of 2 to 1 has often been quoted as the minimum desirable, but a correct ratio depends on the length of the credit terms for receivables as compared to payables and the ease with which inventories can be sold.

Acid Test or Quick Ratio—measures same things as current ratio.

$$\frac{\text{Cash} + \text{Securities} + \text{Receivables}}{\text{Current Liabilities}} = \frac{\$137,000}{\$93,000} = 1.5 \text{ to } 1$$

What has been said above for the current ratio is also true for this ratio. The acid test ratio is considered by many to be better than the current ratio because it eliminates inventories which are not always easily converted into cash. The rule of thumb ratio is 1 to 1.

Accounts Receivable to Sales—measures credit and collection policy effectiveness.

$$\frac{\text{Accounts Receivable}}{\text{Sales}} = \frac{\$99,000}{\$950,000} = 10.4 \text{ percent of sales uncollected}$$

In general, the lower the ratio the better because the faster the accounts receivable are collected the less the chance of bad debt losses and the less capital tied up in accounts receivable. However, more liberal credit terms may result in greatly increased sales and so long as the increased loss from bad debts and the increased cost of capital tied up in receivables is less than the additional net income from the additional sales, it is profitable to allow more liberal credit terms. Accounts receivable should also be aged; that is, a determination should be made of how long they have been outstanding (for example, amount less than 30 days' old, amount from 30–60 days' old, 60–120 days' old, over 120 days' old).

Finished Goods Inventory Turnover—number of times a year inventory must be replaced.

$$\frac{\text{Cost of Goods Sold}}{\text{Average Inventory of Finished Goods}} = \frac{\$685,000}{\$35,500} = 19.3 \text{ times a year}$$

$$\text{Average Inventory} = \frac{\text{Beginning} + \text{Ending Inventory}}{2}$$

$$= \frac{\$33,000 + \$38,000}{2}$$

In general, the larger the number of turnovers the better from the standpoint of safety, capital investment in inventory, and danger of obsolescence loss. However, too high a ratio may result in the loss of customers due to insufficient quantities on hand for proper product selection or delivery delays because of running out of stock. The use of Lifo will distort this ratio.

Raw Material Inventory Turnover

$$\frac{\text{Raw Material Used in Production}}{\text{Average Inventory of Raw Materials}} = \frac{\$234,000}{\$24,500} = 9.6 \text{ times a year}$$

$$\text{Average Inventory} = \frac{\text{Beginning} + \text{Ending Inventory}}{2}$$

$$= \frac{\$23,000 + \$26,000}{2}$$

The same factors are involved as in the case of finished goods.

General Financial Condition Ratios

Owners' Equity to Debt

$$\frac{\text{Net Worth}}{\text{Liabilities}} = \frac{\$507,000}{\$193,000} = 2.6 \text{ to } 1$$

In general, the higher the ratio the more financially secure the company, because greater losses can be incurred before the creditors would lose money and force the company into bankruptcy. However, a greater return on the stockholders' investment can be obtained with a lower ratio if money can be borrowed at low enough interest rates.

Security for Long-Term Debt

$$\frac{\text{Pledged Assets}}{\text{Bonds Payable}} = \frac{\$300,000}{\$100,000} = 3 \text{ to } 1$$

The higher the ratio the safer are the bonds as an investment.

Sales to Fixed Assets

$$\frac{\text{Sales}}{\text{Fixed Assets}} = \frac{\$950,000}{\$300,000} = 3.2 \text{ times}$$

The higher the ratio the less the likelihood of overinvestment in fixed assets or, conversely, the greater the return on fixed assets. Many prefer to use cost of goods sold or manufactured instead of sales to eliminate the effect of profits from the ratio.

Net Worth to Fixed Assets

$$\frac{\text{Net Worth}}{\text{Fixed Assets}} = \frac{\$507,000}{\$300,000} = 1.7 \text{ times}$$

This is another measure of possible overinvestment in fixed assets.

Cautions to Be Exercised in Statement Analysis

There are obviously as many comparisons and ratios to be derived from financial statements as there are combinations of figures. The preceding sections have presented only a few of these with examples of the most useful ones. In undertaking statement analysis, the following cautions should be observed:

1. Avoid meaningless ratios. Many ratios in addition to the above have been suggested, but most have no significance because the figures compared have no significance or relation to each other.
2. Compare related ratios. One may indicate that what is shown by the other is not as significant as at first supposed.
3. Remember that undesirable conditions may bring about some good ratios and vice versa.

4. Remember that undisclosed facts may have a definite bearing on the statements. Financial statements merely show financial facts. They may imply the causes of those facts, but there is no guarantee that the implications are correct.

5. No ratios or percentages should be considered without at the same time considering the figures from which they have been computed.

6. Remember that changes in the percentages in a vertical analysis can be caused by both the numerator and denominator.

7. Horizontal percentage changes must be interpreted in the light of supplementary information. For example, a 25 percent increase in sales does not necessarily justify a 25 percent increase in an expense.

8. Weigh the results of the analysis of a given business against general business conditions and other similar businesses to see whether the changes are better or worse than average.

9. Remember that price level changes are ignored in financial statements, and this fact means that assets other than current, net worth, and depreciation expenses usually do not reflect current values.

Detailed Expense Analysis

Management has the responsibility for overall control of the operations of a business, but the control area of utmost and ultimate importance is profitability. Without continuing profits a company cannot continue to exist. It is this area which commands much of the control time of management. Furthermore, the expenses of operation command most of the control time spent on profitability. The revenues of a company are largely determined by sales effort, product quality, and demand, which require little control in comparison with the expenses. For this reason, expense control will be treated in greater detail.

Responsibility Accounting

In order to have an expense control system it is necessary to fix the responsibility for each expense by proper expense distribution. Expenses must be allocated to the departments which caused them and those which cannot be distributed on any logical basis should not be allocated. The manager of a department must be held responsible for the expenses of operating his department but must not be held accountable for any portion of his department's expense over which he has no control. By way of illustration, it is not uncommon for a manufacturing plant to operate its own power plant. Every operating department will use power generated in this plant but operating department managers should not be held responsible for power costs allocated to their departments. In this example, all power costs should be the responsibility of the manager of the power plant. He is the person who can control costs of operating the power plant.

Having fixed responsibility for each expense, there must be a determination of what amount each expense should be, that is, each manager must be given a norm against which he can compare his actual performance. After making a comparison of actual expenses with "normal" expenses, the causes of any significant differences should be analyzed and, finally, steps should be taken to prevent recurrence of such unfavorable variations.

Expense Budgets

The process of determining what an expense ought to be and establishing a norm is termed "budgeting." In order to budget expenses, it is necessary to know something about expense behavior, that is, how an expense will change in amount relative to other important changes in the operation of a business.

Expenses may be classified into four basic types:

1. *Fixed Expenses*—those which remain the same regardless of volume.
2. *Variable Expenses*—those which vary in direct proportion to some measure of volume such as production quantities, sales revenues, quantity of sales, labor hours, labor cost, orders filled, number of deliveries, mileage, etc.
3. *Semivariable Expenses*—those which vary to some extent but not in direct proportion to some measure of volume such as those listed above. They must be analyzed to determine their exact behavior.
4. *Expenses Set by Management Policy*—for the most part they consist of order-getting costs (advertising, salesmen's salaries). This type is sometimes called Appropriated Expenses. Instead of varying with volume, they cause volume to vary.

Types 1, 2, and 4 in the above classification are ordinarily easy to recognize, but type 3 is generally not only difficult to observe, but, once discovered, is difficult to budget. However, the past behavior of a semivariable expense, once recognized as such, can be initially budgeted with the use of a relatively simple observation technique. Assume that a given company measures its production for a given department in labor hours and makes the following analysis of production and one semivariable expense for two actual months of the current fiscal year:

Month	Hours	Expense
July	60,000	$2,600
December	40,000	2,000
Difference	20,000	$ 600

$600 \div 20,000$ hours $= \$0.03$

Variable Expenses in December: $40,000 \times \$ 0.03 = \$1,200$
Fixed Expense in December: $\$2,000 - \$1,200 = \$ 800$
Expense at any production level: $\$ 800 + \$ 0.03$ per hour

The above technique essentially breaks a semivariable expense into its fixed and variable portions which results in a formula that can be used to determine expected cost at any level of production. It should be emphasized that this technique analyzes past actual expense behavior which may or may not have been efficient. It should be determined whether these actual expenses of the past have been excessive by the following techniques:

1. Comparison with the expenses of other companies both in total and percentages.
2. Analysis, experimentation, and consultations with employees.
3. Time and motion study.

Appropriated Expenses

The preceding control techniques are designed to control all expenses that can be classified as variable, semivariable, or fixed. These expenses include all manufacturing expenses, order-filling distribution expenses, and all other operating expenses except appropriated expenses, which are set by management policy. Appropriated expenses are those which are found primarily among order-getting expenses. Some examples include advertising, sales promotion, product research, and market research expenses. Appropriated expenses present a special problem in that cause and effect relationship to volume is just the opposite of other expenses, that is, these expenses *cause* sales instead of being caused by them. It is, therefore, not a question of keeping them as low as possible, but rather one of determining the proper amount required to achieve the objectives set. Control of this type of expense is obtained through an appropriation budget. This type of budget merely establishes an amount that will be incurred for a given type of effort (advertising) and adheres to this amount throughout the specified period. An appropriation budget is very much like the budget a family might use to control expenditures, and, thus, does not present a very difficult analysis problem.

Effects of Varying Expense Behavior

Before turning to more sophisticated control systems used to control unappropriated expenses, the effects of differing expense behavior will be illustrated. Expense behavior can have an important effect upon management decisions, with respect to unit cost and pricing. The following exhibit might prove important to such decisions.

EFFECT OF PRODUCTION QUANTITIES ON UNIT COST

Exhibit I

| | QUARTER | | | | |
	1st	2d	3d	4th	Total
Production Quantity in Units of Product	20,000	30,000	40,000	50,000	140,000
Fixed Expense	$ 6,000	$ 6,000	$ 6,000	$ 6,000	$ 24,000
Variable Expense	5,000	7,500	10,000	12,500	35,000
Total Expense	$11,000	$13,500	$16,000	$18,500	$ 59,000
Fixed Expense per Unit	$ 0.30	$ 0.20	$ 0.15	$ 0.12	$ 0.17
Variable Expense per Unit	0.25	0.25	0.25	0.25	0.25
Total Expense per Unit	$ 0.55	$ 0.45	$ 0.40	$ 0.37	$ 0.42

To further illustrate how the different behavioral characteristics of expenses might affect management decisions, a "direct costing" income statement of Specialty Products Company for 1966 is presented in Exhibit J. An income statement in this form shows the contribution each product line is making to the overall profit of a company. In constructing it, the revenues from the sale of each product line are first determined. Secondly, all expenses directly attributable to each line are deducted. It is important to note that the terms "variable" and "direct" are not synonymous. Direct expenses are apt to be primarily variable but would include all semivariable and fixed expenses that are directly attributable to a given product line. Deducting direct expenses from sales of each line gives the contribution to overall profit of each line, that is, if any one of the lines were dropped by a company the net loss (or gains if the contribution is negative) to profit would be the amount of the line's contribution to the covering of fixed costs and profit, assuming no change in the outcome of any other product line. This is true because the indirect expenses are those that are common to all lines and would not necessarily be affected by the dropping of any given line.

SPECIALTY PRODUCTS COMPANY

STATEMENT OF INCOME BY PRODUCT LINE
For Year Ended December 31, 1966

Exhibit J

	Line A	Line B	Line C	Total
Gross Sales	$420,000	$360,000	$190,000	$970,000
Sales Returns and Allowances	10,000	6,000	4,000	20,000
Net Sales	$410,000	$354,000	$186,000	$950,000
Direct Expenses				
Manufacturing	$250,000	$200,000	$100,000	$550,000
Selling	20,000	16,000	20,000	56,000
Administrative	4,000	9,000	3,000	16,000
Contribution toward Covering Fixed Expenses and Profit	$136,000	$129,000	$ 63,000	$328,000
Indirect Expenses				
Manufacturing				$135,000
Selling				90,000
Administrative				55,000
Total				$280,000
Net Income from Operations				$ 48,000
Other Income and Expense (net)				6,400
Net Income before Income Tax				$ 41,600
Federal Income Tax				15,600
Net Income				$ 26,000

The income analysis appearing in Exhibit J is relatively new, having appeared after World War II, and is gaining in popularity with company managements. The more basic relationships presented in Exhibit I have been recognized by managements for many decades. These are just two examples of the effect upon operations of differing expense behavior but they should serve to emphasize the point that expense analysis is an important aspect of managerial control of profitability.

Manufacturing Overhead Budgeting

Previously it was stated that in order to control any given expense it was necessary to know what the expense ought to be. The determination of what an expense ought to be was illustrated and the outcome was termed a budget. The observation that is illustrated on page 75 can be used for any single expense category or the total expense of a given department or unit of a firm, but finds its greatest use in controlling manufacturing expenses that don't fall into the category of direct (variable) labor and direct (variable) materials. These indirect manufacturing expenses are often referred to as manufacturing overhead and a "semivariable overhead budget" is often used to control them. This type of budget appears in Exhibit K. In this example, the manufacturing operations of Specialty Products Company are used as an illustration. The budget would be the expected total amount of overhead expense at any level of production or $10,000 plus $4 for every machine-hour worked in the plant. Specialty Products Company is considered to have several products and product lines and, therefore, production is measured in machine-hours rather than units of product. It is further assumed that the company determined this budget by applying the technique illustrated earlier and adjusted it for changes necessitated by further analysis of the manufacturing operation.

The use of such an overhead budget allows a company to do two things:

1. Cost the product as it is completed rather than after an operating period is completed.

2. Control the cost of manufacturing overhead.

Costing the product is effected with the use of the burden rate. This rate is not always completely accurate, but it enables a firm to estimate overhead cost per unit of product manufactured. Control over manufacturing expenses is effected by the resulting variances which tell the manager the cause of any efficiency or inefficiency. Generally, the performance variance is the one of importance to management because it represents inefficiencies in the price and usage of overhead items which can be controlled. The volume variance, on the other hand, represents the difference between the actual experience and the expected experience because actual production volume was different than expected production volume. This volume variance can be corrected only by additional sales and is due to the fact that some of the manufacturing overhead expense is fixed (amounting to $10,000 a month in this case).

COST BUDGETING AND CONTROL

The Specialty Products Company employs a semivariable budget to control manufacturing overhead. It was estimated that fixed costs would be $10,000 per month, and variable costs would be $40,000 per month at a normal level of production. This variable cost was based on a level of production of 10,000 machine hours at $4 per hour.

During the month of June 1966, the actual machine hours were 9,500 and the actual overhead incurred was $51,500.

1. The burden rate = ($10,000 + $40,000) ÷ 10,000 = $5 per machine-hour
2. The total absorbed cost for June = $9,500 × 5 = $47,500
3. Overhead underabsorbed = $4,000

Actual Overhead	$51,500
Absorbed Overhead	47,500
Underabsorbed	$ 4,000

4. The total overhead budgeted = $10,000 + (4 × $9,500) = $48,000
   ("Budgeted" refers to the amount which would have been budgeted had the company known what the actual production level would be.)
5. The volume variance = $500 (unfavorable)
   (Budgeted overhead minus absorbed overhead equals volume variance)
6. The performance variance = $3,500 (unfavorable)
   (Budgeted overhead minus actual overhead equals performance variance)

Standard Cost Systems

Semivariable overhead budgets provide excellent indicators of areas where control is needed in manufacturing overhead. Semi-variable budgets are designed, however, for expenses that behave in a semivariable fashion, and not for expenses that are variable in behavior. Standard cost systems are used often for this latter purpose. The term "standard" is approximately synonymous with "budget," and a standard cost is the amount a given expense ought to be. Budgets, however, are determined at least initially from past expense behavior while standards are usually derived from time and motion and engineering studies.

Any variable expense could be controlled by the use of a standard cost system, but here again these systems find their greatest application to manufacturing costs; in this instance, direct labor and direct material. Such a system is predicated on the assumption that one ought to be able to determine with precision the amount of labor and primary materials necessary to produce any given unit of product and, further, that one ought to be able to determine the price of these inputs. The figures produced by a standard cost system represent a breakdown of the difference between total standard cost for a period and actual cost for a period. This difference is analyzed by cause. Since volume cannot enter into the difference when an expense is variable, the cause of any efficiency or inefficiency can be traced to either a price different than standard or quantity usage different than standard.

Exhibit L is an example of the use of standard costs. It was assumed for purposes of this exhibit that Specialty Products Company has a production department for one of the special products it manufactures and that standards have been determined by engineering and time and motion studies. An overhead budget has been included in the illustration to demonstrate that it can be combined with standard costs to provide overall control over a department of a firm.

USE OF STANDARD COSTS

Specialty Products Company uses a standard cost system to control costs in one Special product department and has established the following standards for a standard level of production of 10,000 units per month:

	Standards		Standard Cost per Unit
Materials	Quantity per unit	5 lbs.	
	Price per pound	$2.00	$10.00
Labor	Time per unit	10 hours	
	Wage rate	$4 per hour	40.00
Overhead	Fixed cost per month	$5,000	
	Variable rate	$0.45 per hour	4.50
	Total Standard Cost per Unit		$54.50

Actual data for the month of July 1966, is as follows:

Material purchased and used	45,200 pounds at $2.02 per pound
Actual production	9,000 units
Labor used	89,600 hours at $3.95 per hour
Actual overhead incurred	$40,000

Variances are computed as follows:

1. Material purchase price variance = $904 (unfavorable) [(Actual price minus standard price) × Actual material purchased] [($2.02 − $2.00) × 45,200 lbs.] = $904. The variance is unfavorable because the actual price was higher than standard.

2. Material usage variance = $400 (unfavorable) [(Actual usage minus standard usage) × Standard price] [(45,200 lbs. − 45,000 lbs.) × $2.00] = $400. The variance is unfavorable because actual usage exceeded standard usage.

3. Wage rate variance = $4,480 (favorable) (Computed in the same way as material purchase variance) [($4 − $3.95) × 89,600 hours] = $4,480. The variance is favorable because the average actual wage rate was less than standard.

4. Labor usage variance = $1,600 (favorable) (Computed in the same way as material usage variance) [(90,000 hours − 89,600 hours) × $4 = $1,600. The variance is favorable because actual usage was less than standard usage.

In order to illustrate the control information provided by a standard cost system, a few examples from Exhibit L will be taken. First, the company experienced an unfavorable material purchase price variance due to the fact that material cost $0.02 per pound more than it should have cost. The manager could use this information to go to the purchasing department and ask why this occurred. Perhaps material specifications or demand have changed and, therefore, the standard should be changed. On the other hand, it is possible that the material was not purchased in an economical quantity, with a resulting increase in price, and the purchasing department should be made aware that it should attempt to do better in the future.

The labor usage variance provides another good example of information provided by standard costs. This variance amounted to $1,600 and was favorable, that is, less labor was used to manufacture the 9,000 units than was thought probable. Even though this variance is favorable, it should be investigated by the manager. He may find that the standard is faulty and needs revision, or he may find that quality was sacrificed for quantity. Generally, when there is any significant variance from standard, some correction for future operations is possible and the variance should be investigated.

Value Analysis

Budgets and standard costs offer effective control techniques within the constraints of fixed objectives and resources. Another technique which helps to control expenditures but, in a broader systems context, is value analysis. The federal government first applied this approach to the military spending section of the national budget in an attempt to provide greater benefits to the taxpayer at less cost. Implementation of value analysis programs requires that experienced personnel study high price and high volume items in an effort to lower their purchase cost without sacrificing quality and reliability. This definition appears quite similar to that of industrial engineering which seeks to improve methods and/or materials but really extends much beyond since the value analysts adopt a systems view. They consider not only the product (or service) itself but also the function of the product, the users of the product, and possible substitutes for the product.

The manager who is interested in applying the value analysis technique must answer the following questions.

1. What are the highest cost items or processes for which I have responsibility and authority?

2. What is the primary function of these items?
3. What else are these items used for?
4. Is there something else that can do the job that would be acceptable to the user?
5. What would be the cost of the substitute?
6. Are experienced personnel available who can analyze these items in depth and also design or find a source of supply for the substitute?

Organizational control for value analysis might best be accomplished through a matrix approach whereby specialists are assigned to projects on a temporary basis. For example, a value analysis team consisting of a senior engineer, purchasing agent, and production supervisor might be given the responsibility for evaluating high-cost, low-margin components to determine if any of them could be purchased outside less expensively than produced internally. These experts might apply their skills to the problem for only one hour each day for as long as it takes to reach a conclusion. In this manner, an integrated systems attack would probably lead to a more complete selection and evaluation of alternatives and ultimately to more effective decisions.

As an example of a much smaller scale application of value analysis, consider the university department head who is in search of methods to reduce his expenditures for office supplies. He begins by looking at the items which represent the greatest cost, and finds that one of the highest cost items is manila file folders. He queries his secretaries and office suppliers about their use of these folders and the possibility of substitutes. He finds that a product is available which serves the same function as the traditional folder, costs twice as much per unit, but lasts four times as long. Consequently, an immediate changeover is made and the overall cost of this item for a four-year period is reduced by 100 percent.

Examples like the above probably occur very frequently but it is the aggressive manager taking the initiative and causing change who most consistently demonstrates effective control. By so doing, this type of manager does not rely upon luck, but, in fact, places the odds for success in his favor and improves his "promotability" with each value analyzed cost reduction.

Summary

This chapter has attempted an overview of control through the use of financial statements and accounting analyses. The primary use of these tools is profitability control, although liquidity and general financial condition control are also obtained through them. Profitability can be controlled at the firm level through the use of vertical, horizontal, and ratio analysis. With these general tools, the manager can observe the relationships between different parts of the overall operation and maintain, therefore, overall control.

Within subdivisions of a firm, managers must concern themselves with control of individual expenses. In order to exercise control over an expense or a department's total expense, budgets must be used to compare with actual experience in order to know whether or not a given operation is efficient. Semivariable overhead budgets and standard cost systems are useful techniques for gaining information necessary to control individual and department expenses.

CHAPTER FIVE

Graphic Controls

Graphic methods are widely used for organization control. A graphic control method is a pictorial representation of data, made for the purpose of communicating information, facilitating decision-making, and motivating efforts toward the attainment of planned objectives. Systems personnel use graphic models as a basis for analyses, to isolate problems, to identify duplications and delays, and to present and sell new ideas to top management.

Graphic controls may be dynamic or static. A dynamic control is used for an on-going process. It is posted periodically, and decisions are made as a result of that posting. In essence, the control feeds back information to the decision-maker, who either makes changes in the system to bring it back on course, or decides that it is satisfactory, and makes no change. Dynamic control charts usually have *time* as the independent variable.

A static control is established either at the beginning (during the planning stage) of a run or sequence of events, or at the end. A static control established at the beginning may originate as part of the analytical work required to establish an objective. Once the goal is established, the control is used as a reference which alerts the manager when points of departure from the original plan occur. A new decision may then be required to depart or not to depart from the original plan. With this approach, the decision is made from the vantage point of the original thinking and planning on the subject, rather than by whim or happenstance, as will occur in uncontrolled processes.

A static control established at the end of an event cannot control what has already been done, but will be useful for making decisions regarding future events of a similar nature.

The type and number of graphic controls which can be used are limited only by the imagination of the user. This chapter will illustrate those which have proved to be most useful.

Dynamic Controls

Five broad classifications of dynamic controls which are commonly used will be discussed in the following order.

1. Gantt charts
2. Program Evaluation and Review Techniques (PERT)
3. Statistical quality control charts
4. Line charts
5. Goal-seeking charts

Gantt Charts

The Gantt chart is perhaps the oldest, yet most commonly used, graphic control method. Essentially, the Gantt chart consists of a series of horizontal bars, each representing a given amount of planned accomplishment over a specified period. Below each bar is a second contrasting bar representing actual accomplishment, as of a certain date. Thus, a glance will reveal whether a product is ahead of schedule, behind schedule, or on schedule.

The Gantt approach can be used to chart any conceivable endeavor that has been planned and which requires time to accomplish. Such diverse activities as conducting a sales campaign, building a factory, establishing a budget for the coming year, or developing a new product have all been controlled with the Gantt chart.

An example will illustrate the principle. The Jones Job Shop, Inc., manufactures to customer order. Each order is different, requiring

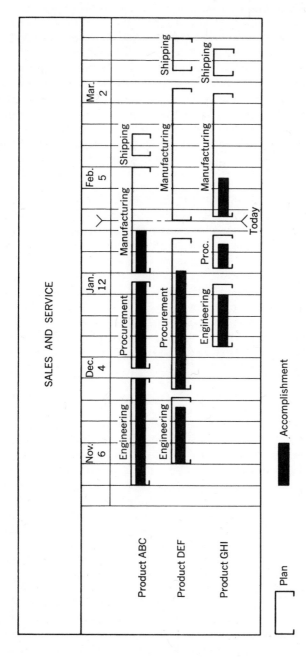

Figure 5-1 Gantt Chart for Sales and Service

time for engineering, procurement, manufacturing, and shipping. Figures 5-1, 5-2, and 5-3 show how Gantt charts might appear in sales and service, engineering, and manufacturing, respectively.[1]

The chart in sales and service reveals that products ABC and DEF are behind schedule. Inspection of product GHI reveals that manufacturing has started, even though both engineering and procurement are behind schedule. This is not unusual in a real situation, but can also be the beginning of needless expense. The charts indicate this potentially troublesome situation within sufficient time to allow management to take steps to bring the departments back on schedule before orders begin missing shipping dates.

The Gantt chart in engineering, Figure 5-2, indicates that tool design and gauge design may be causing some trouble. There is little need for a change here, because both will probably be caught up within two to three weeks, if no rush jobs are received. A real bottleneck is product drafting, which is also three weeks behind schedule but is backlogged for three months. Additional staffing or overtime will probably be necessary here.

To understand manufacturing's problem, look at its Operation Route Sheet, Table 5-1. Let us assume that the Jones Job Shop has an order for 8,000 of product ABC. This product is made up of two parts, A and B, which are assembled to become the completed product, ABC.

For reasons not revealed, production control has scheduled the manufacture of product ABC on machines 1, 2, 3, 4, and 5, with machines 1, 2, and 3 used on both components A and B. We note

TABLE 5-1 / Operation Route Sheet, Product ABC

	Operation Number	Operation	Machine Number	Production (pcs/hr)
Component A:	A-1	Drill	1	240
	A-2	Drill	2	250
	A-3	Mill	3	175
	A-4	Turn	4	250
Component B:	B-1	Mill	3	100
	B-2	Drill	2	200
	B-3	Drill	1	280
	B-4	Mill	5	100
Assembly ABC:	C-1	Assemble A&B	Bench	200

---

[1] Other departments, such as procurement, shipping, personnel, and finance, could have similar charts concerning their own phase of the overall problem.

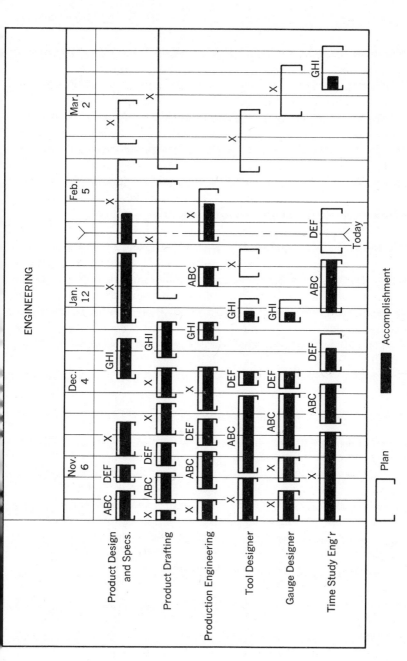

Figure 5-2 Gantt Chart for Engineering Department

Plan

Accomplishment

87

that operation B-1 is a day behind schedule. This is not serious since the schedule has left a day of slack between operations B-1 and A-3 on machine number 3, where this problem will be resolved. Thus, no action is necessary at this time.

Notice that in these examples, Figures 5-1, 5-2, and 5-3, each job reveals percentage of accomplishment as of a certain date. If it is desirable to know why a delay occurred, the *actual* time spent doing the job is plotted on the actual day when the time was spent. Figure 5-3 might then look like Figure 5-4, called a Machine Record. Similar charts could also be maintained, recording delays related to employee time or to material availability.

Gantt charts are extremely useful as control tools. A note of caution is in order, however. It is possible to get so enamored with charting techniques that the tail begins to wag the dog. An ammunition manufacturer at one time was maintaining 400 separate Gantt charts on various products. The plant was about six months behind in its promises. Examination revealed that the control people were six weeks behind in posting the charts and were turning all their energies toward making nice-looking charts and ignoring the realities of schedules.

Program Evaluation and Review Techniques (PERT)

Certain managerial problems involve hundreds of separate activities, some of which must be worked upon concurrently and others which must be completed prior to succeeding activities. Such projects as plant construction, new product development, installation of a computer system, or movement into new facilities require detailed planning. Information about the degree of completion and cumulated costs must be provided on a continuing basis so that the projects can be effectively controlled. Gantt charts are not the most effective control method for such complicated projects.

A widely publicized and most practical addition to the executive's tool kit of control methods is known as the Program Evaluation and Review Technique or PERT, and is applicable to a variety of complex problem situations. PERT enables management to employ more scientific planning before initiating lengthy projects but, most important, it provides improved management control once the project has begun. It provides accurate means for progress reporting, identification of problem areas, management of human and capital re-

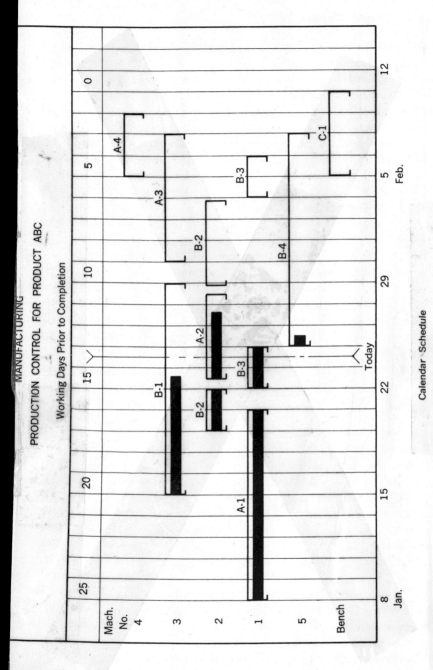

Figure 5-3 Gantt Chart for Manufacturing

89

sources, and allows for better communications, decision-making, and time savings.

PERT was originally conceived in 1959 when the Office of Naval Research and Lockheed Aircraft Corporation found traditional control methods lacking since they did not provide for cost calculations and efficient shifting of resources to speed up segments of the project which were behind schedule. The PERT model was first applied to the Polaris Weapon System contract and is said to have contributed significantly to a two-year reduction in the completion time of the project.

PERT project control requires that each distinct activity of a planned project be identified and placed in its proper sequence. That is, each activity should be specified in terms of those activities which must precede and those which must follow it before the project is totally completed. This sequence of activities is then represented in graphic form by means of a network of lines and nodes as shown in Figure 5-5. This figure might represent the installation of a computer system, where A signifies the beginning of the project, B the completion of a training program for key-punch operators, and C the completion of an air-conditioned equipment room. Activities leading toward events B and C are independent of one another and are therefore shown as occurring simultaneously, but each must be completed before activities leading toward events D and E can be initiated. The time required to complete the activity for event B is represented by three estimates, one, two, and five weeks, shown on the activity line between A and B. Determination and use of these time estimates are explained later in this section.

PERT analysis involves detailed and often costly planning and implementation and is usually not applied to small projects extending for short time durations. According to Timms,[2] "Usually only complex projects involving many activities with uncertain completion times warrant the use of formal PERT networking." However, even in relatively simple situations, PERT philosophy can be helpful in bringing to the attention of the manager those activities and relationships which must be controlled in order to accomplish a project objective. In such instances it would probably be sufficient to construct a network similar to the one shown in Figure 5-5 without including the time estimates.

---

[2] H. L. Timms, *The Production Function in Business* (Homewood, Ill.: Richard D. Irwin, Inc., 1966), p. 210.

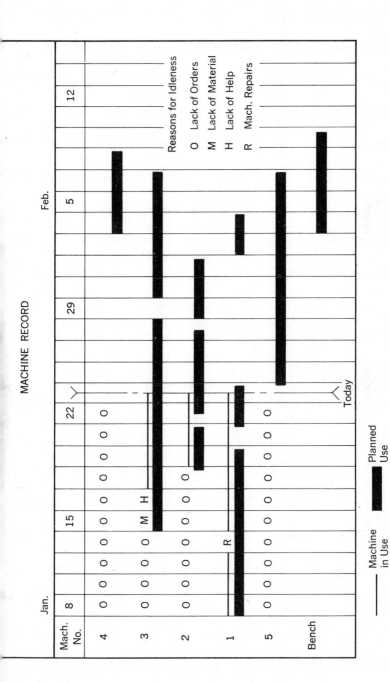

Figure 5-4 Gantt Chart Showing Machine Utilization and Cause of Downtime

91

For the standard PERT analysis, however, time estimates are normally required after the activities have been identified and sequenced. These estimates should be obtained from those personnel who are directly associated with the activities, for theirs is likely to be the closest approximation. For example, if testing of a prototype is one activity in a new product development project, the chief of quality control or chief inspector should be consulted regarding the time it will take to perform the necessary tests.

Three time estimates are usually obtained for each activity. The first is considered the *optimistic* time and is that time associated with near perfect conditions. In other words, if everything goes right (which seldom happens in modern organizations), the optimistic time will be realized. Another time estimate is obtained and classified as the *most likely* time to complete an activity, and, finally, the *pessimistic* time is estimated. It is that amount of time required to complete an activity when almost nothing goes right. A formula is then applied to these three estimates to arrive at what is commonly called the "expected" time for the activity. An example is presented to clarify this procedure. The quality control chief estimated that he

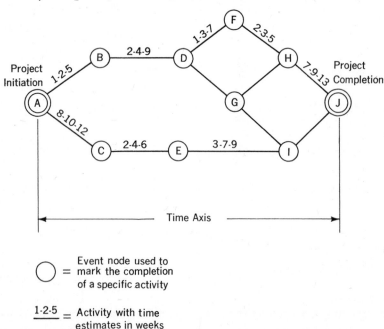

Figure 5-5 PERT Activity Network

could completely check out the prototype in one week under ideal conditions. Such inspections would normally run about two weeks, and that bad weather might extend the job by three weeks above the normal. A PERT analyst would calculate the expected time for the inspection as follows:

$$\text{Expected time} = \frac{\text{Pessimistic} + 4 \text{ Most likely} + \text{Optimistic}}{6}$$

$$= \frac{1 + (4 \times 2) + 5}{6}$$

$$= 2\tfrac{1}{3} \text{ weeks}$$

This calculation is based upon the Beta Distribution and, as the reader will note, the most likely estimate is weighted the heaviest but, at the same time, allowance is made for possible pessimistic and optimistic conditions.

Once expected time estimates have been determined for all activities in the network, the total time required to complete the project can be calculated. This time is represented in the network by the sequence of dependent times which has the greatest total. This sequence usually is referred to as the *critical path,* since the project completion time is directly dependent upon the time length of this path. For effective control, management must watch the critical path most carefully since any delay in the time required to complete an activity in this path means a corresponding delay in the project completion time.

Any path other than the critical path is referred to as a "slack path" since it will require less time to complete the slack path than the critical path. Discovery of slack in a project is most helpful since management can often reduce project completion times by shifting resources (men and equipment) from the slack paths into the critical path activities.

A Central Pennsylvania construction company is involved in large-scale projects demanding the use of men and equipment at various work sites located over a stretch of interstate highway. The contractor has one man constantly assigned to PERT control of his contracts. He has been able to make more efficient use of resources, especially large earth moving equipment, which, for many road contractors, has a tendency to be in the right spots at the wrong times.

Interim status reports provide management with feedback information relative to the progress on its projects. Comparisons are made between scheduled and actual performance with special attention directed to the critical path. As activities progress toward completion, circumstances may alter the critical path; that is, as delays occur in the slack paths and optimistic times are realized in the critical path, what was once a slack path may suddenly turn into the critical project path and management's attention is alerted accordingly through PERT project control. To eliminate unnecessary hand computations, larger companies have a computer program which calculates the critical path on a daily basis for complex projects involving thousands of interrelated activities.

Several variations of the basic PERT control technique have been introduced since the successful completion of the Polaris. Probably the most publicized of these is known as CPM or Critical Path Method and utilizes the same approach to project planning but, instead of placing emphasis on completion *time*, it places emphasis upon project *cost*. Naturally, in developing a weapons system, time is of the essence but, in many managerial situations, time can be sacrificed in favor of reduced costs and the CPM Method permits management to inspect various alternative project proposals in the light of their opposing costs.

Implementation of a PERT-COST system begins in the same manner as does the PERT-TIME Method. A graphic flow chart is constructed showing the relationships among all activities and events required to complete the project. However, when considering costs, it is necessary to determine two separate estimates for each branch in the network, such as (1) the minimum time for an activity and its cost and (2) the minimum cost for an activity and its time. The same method of providing three estimates (optimistic, pessimistic, and most likely) is applied to both the times and the costs. A critical path is then developed using the minimum costs of activities throughout the network instead of the minimum times. The completion date under minimum cost conditions may be too far in the future to accept and, consequently, substitutes will be required. When this is the case, detailed analyses are made of all resources so that alternative means can be applied to selected activities to reduce their completion times. For example, it might be necessary to shift several graders from one road site representing an activity with positive slack (extra time available without delaying the completion of the total project) to another site representing negative slack (delay in critical path) even though the total cost for grading the two sites is increased. This method of dealing with time-cost combinations is not optimum in terms of minimizing either time or cost but does represent a scientific approach to a compromise which meets the needs of a given situation.

A simple heuristic (search reducing technique) which the reader may wish to keep in mind relevant to PERT-COST analysis is that compromises should be made within those activities which promise the greatest savings to the total system. To determine which activities offer this advantage, consult the critical path and select those activities for which the ratio of increasing cost to decreasing time is the smallest. If those activities for which this ratio is smallest are selected, the analyst has the best chance of developing an effective compromise.

Recent developments in computer output devices have increased the manager's graphic control capabilities. Automated display systems have been designed which can provide graphic information on screens and, in certain instances, it is possible for the manager to manipulate the information portrayed on the screen by using a keyboard or a light pen. A systems manager, for example, could view a complete PERT network and alter various activities within the network in order to determine the effects on resources, slack times, or even total project completion time. In this type of interaction, the computer serves as a lightning quick calculator and decision tool for the executive.

Statistical Quality Control Charts

Industrial statisticians in the past 40 years have developed a kind of graphic control for product quality. These are generally known as statistical quality control charts, or SQC charts, but the principle behind the construction of these charts is so basic that the approach can be used wherever a continuous process is performed that needs to be controlled. In fact, they have been used as controls for traffic accidents, manufacturing capability, raw material costs, grievances, personnel turnover, et cetera.

The theoretical basis of SQC charts is simple.[3] Most continuing processes tend to settle into some routine. If a characteristic of the process can be measured periodically, and reduced to numbers, a control chart of that process can be constructed. The characteristic might be daily or weekly sales, auto accidents per day, dimensions of a manufactured part in 0.001 inches, numbers of defective pieces in a lot, resignations or grievances per month, and so forth.

---

[3] Background in probability theory is necessary for full understanding of this subject. See E. L. Grant, *Statistical Quality Control*, 3d edition. New York: McGraw-Hill Book Company, 1964.

To construct a control chart, it is necessary to know where the data center, how much they vary, and something about their patterns of distribution.

The most useful measure of where the data center (measure of central tendency) is called the *mean.* A similar measure of variability is called the *standard deviation.* Although the pattern of distribution may be unknown, by taking samples of two or more items and averaging them, a distribution for which data are available results, called the Normal Distribution. Even though the distribution of the data is not normal, the distribution of sample *means* taken from these data will approach normality as the sample size gets larger.

These data are then plotted, as shown in Figure 5-6A, with variability plotted vertically and time horizontally. Once about 25 of these points have been plotted, it is possible to calculate limits[4] (shown in Figure 5-6A as UCL and LCL, the Upper Control Limit and Lower Control Limit) for the system. When all 25 points are within these limits, there is a very high probability that the process is in control.

Once it is known that the process is "in control," it is capable of being controlled.[5] After process capability has been demonstrated, any point that goes outside the control limits is considered as being "out of control." This means that something different or abnormal has happened. By investigating the out-of-control point, it may be possible to identify and eliminate the cause of the abnormality.

The three basic types of SQC charts are shown in Figure 5-6.

The x chart, or chart of means of sample size, shows a gradual drift (a) toward the UCL. Then, one point goes "out of control" (heavy X). The operator corrects the process (b), perhaps by adjusting the machine.[6]

The p chart (percentage defective chart) shows gradually improving quality. Where one out of ten initially was defective on the average, it can be seen that the average is now less than six out of 100.

The c chart, bottom of Figure 5-6, shows the number of defects per unit measured. This is useful where hundreds of defects are

---

[4] Usually three standard deviations of the mean away from the mean in each direction.

[5] Bringing a process under control is often the major purpose of a control system.

[6] An important point is that "out of control" does not mean "out of specification." The upper specification limit could be 1.060, and the danger of producing poor quality averted before any poor work is actually produced.

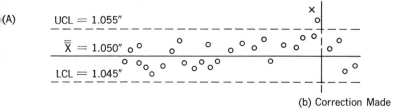

(b) Correction Made

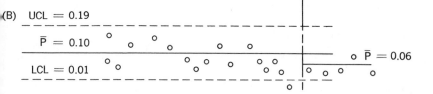

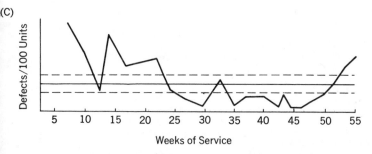

Figure 5-6 Samples of Statistical Quality Control Charts
(A) x Chart. Each point is the average of n measurements (B) p Chart—Percentage Defective. On the average one part in ten parts is defective (C) c Chart—Defects per Unit. Data are plotted according to length of time on the job

possible per unit, such as in electronic equipment, a floor rug, or yard goods. This chart shows the end result of a study to determine the source of trouble on wired panels. Each point represents the work of a different operator, and shows capability versus weeks of service. The tentative conclusion would be that after 43 or 44 weeks, it would be possible to estimate process capability. It also indicates that further investigation is needed to determine why quality drops for operators with longest service.

Line Charts

Simple line charts are perhaps the most common kind of graphic control. Figures 5-7 to 5-9 show typical examples. A line chart used for control purposes will show one or more characteristics plotted vertically, and time plotted horizontally.

The control may be one of three types:

1. Actual versus plan
2. Actual, this year versus last year
3. Progress only, versus some intuitive concept of what progress should be

These are listed from top to bottom in the order of control strength.

Figure 5-7 shows planned ship construction against actual.[7] The control exerted could be improved by plotting standard hours of work planned versus standard hours completed, week by week, rather than percent completed.

Figure 5-8 shows the amount of detail and information that can be communicated by line charts. Where a number of executives must meet to consider a complex project, a presentation comprised of similar charts from all critical control areas will give the total group the same information very rapidly. Although such an array of data appears confusing at first glance, careful presentation of it will help to unify the consideration of a complex problem.

In these figures, strong emphasis is placed on history. In addition, the *plan* (objective) is highlighted (Figure 5-8) by placing a triangle at the desired goal.

Figure 5-9 shows improvement over time.[8] By keeping a graph of man-hours per unit, the progressive improvement is apparent. This type of control operates on the exception principle, indicating where further effort to reduce cost may well be desirable. A product for which cost stays level or increases might warrant further efforts to reduce cost. A product that shows a reasonably steady downward trend would usually be considered satisfactory.

---

[7] G. B. Carson, *Production Handbook*, 2d ed. New York: Ronald Press, 1958, pp. 3–17.

[8] H. B. Maynard, *Industrial Engineering Handbook*. New York: McGraw-Hill Book Company, 1956, pp. 8–250 (data only).

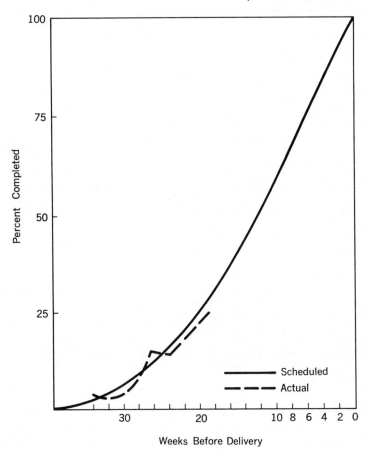

Figure 5-7 Scheduled versus Actual Progress on Ship Construction

SOURCE: *Production Handbook,* Second Edition, edited by Gordon B. Carson. Copyright © 1958, The Ronald Press Company, New York.

Goal-seeking Charts

Goal-seeking charts, as shown in Figure 5-10, are self-explanatory. They serve to keep important goals in mind, and should be located where traffic is heaviest. Industrially, they are particularly effective on safety campaigns, where the goal being sought is to stay unhurt, or at least alive. During World War II, defense bond drives usually set as their goal 100 percent participation, and this kind of chart was common.

A most effective goal-seeking technique was used by Andrew Carnegie in the early twentieth century. The story is told that while

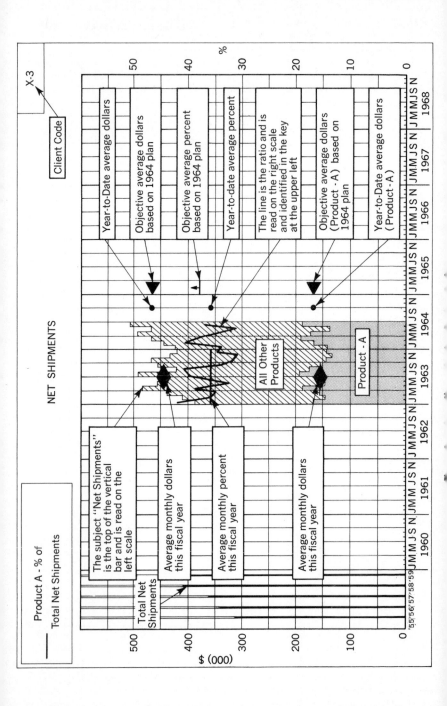

NET SHIPMENTS

Client Code

X-3

%

Product A - % of
Total Net Shipments

Total Net Shipments

Year-to-Date average dollars

Objective average dollars based on 1964 plan

Objective average percent based on 1964 plan

Year-to-date average percent

The line is the ratio and is read on the right scale and identified in the key at the upper left

Objective average dollars (Product - A) based on 1964 plan

Year-to-Date average dollars (Product - A)

The subject "Net Shipments" is the top of the vertical bar and is read on the left scale

Average monthly dollars this fiscal year

Average monthly percent this fiscal year

Average monthly dollars this fiscal year

All Other Products

Product - A

$ (000)

'55'56'57'58'59

1960 1961 1962 1963 1964 1965 1966 1967 1968

walking through a shop one day, he asked the men how many heats they expected to do. When told 8, he took a piece of chalk and wrote a big "8" on the wall. The night crew, when asking and being informed of the meaning of the "8," decided they could do better, and at the end of their shift proudly replaced the "8" with a "10." The day shift, in turn, reacted with a "12." The competition, and the story, ended at an all-time high of "16."

This kind of competitive drive is useful for short runs, but is more difficult to maintain over the long haul.

Static Controls

The static controls discussed here are:

Break-even charts	Wage classification charts
Travel charts	Histograms
Flow charts	Pictorial charts
Organization charts	Linear responsibility charts

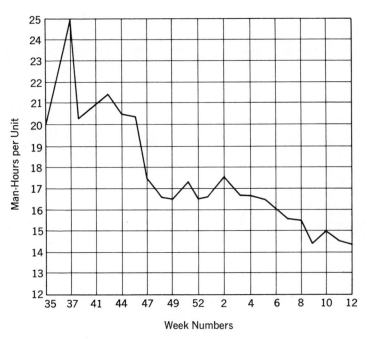

Figure 5-9 Line Chart Showing Progressive Improvement

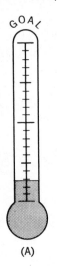

(A)

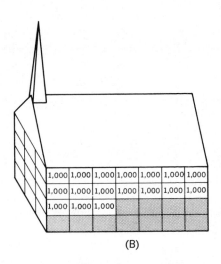

(B)

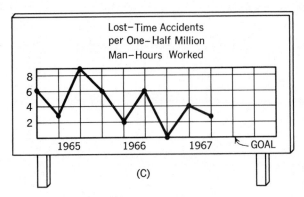

(C)

Figure 5-10 Goal-Seeking Charts

(A) Community Fund Drive (B) Building Campaigns (C) Safety Drives

Break-even Charts

The break-even chart, Figure 5-11, gives an executive a financial picture of his operation. By drawing a vertical line at any point in the graph, a quick, visual profit and loss statement can be determined simply by measuring the vertical lengths of the line segments. For instance, line A develops the following data:

Sales		$420,000
Fixed Costs	$320,000	
Variable Costs	120,000	440,000
Loss		$ 20,000

Line B develops the following data:

Sales		$720,000
Fixed Costs	$320,000	
Variable Costs	220,000	540,000
Gross Profit		180,000
Taxes		30,000
Net Profit		$150,000

If more detail is desired, fixed and variable costs could each be broken down further and plotted. The components of fixed costs might be depreciation on property, depreciation on equipment, salaries of key personnel, interest on borrowed money, floor space expense, and real estate expenses. The components of variable costs might be direct labor, direct material, transportation, and variable overhead.

The executive can use the break-even chart to predict the effect of changes of various kinds in the overall profit picture of his business. An increase in material cost or direct labor, a decrease in sales price in an effort to increase volume, or the purchase of an expensive

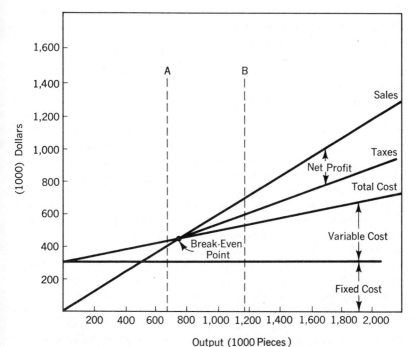

Figure 5-11   Break-even Chart for a Manufacturing Concern

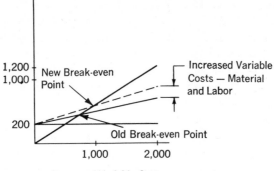

Increased Variable Cost

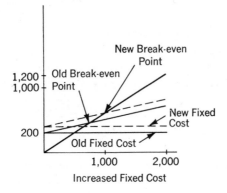

Increased Fixed Cost

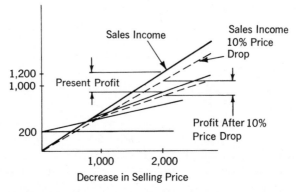

Decrease in Selling Price

Figure 5-12 Changes in Break-even Point due to Various Changes in Operating Expenses

piece of equipment can be pictured quickly on the break-even chart.

Figure 5-12 shows the effect of such changes in the break-even point for no gain, no loss. Such break-even charts assume linear relationships among all variables and the reader should remember that, in the event nonlinear functions are involved, this type of analysis may lead to erroneous conclusions.

Travel Charts

A travel chart is used to analyze the movement of material between different machines or departments. The objective is to determine if the cost of material handling can be reduced by a rearrangement of equipment.

In Figure 5-13A, the figures are representative of the volume of traffic between two points.[9] Thus, the 100 at the intersection of A and H represents 10 times the traffic as does the 10 at the intersection of A and J. If the distance between departments is considered to be roughly proportional to the distance between the letters on the chart, it is apparent that the departments between which the heaviest traffic occurs should be closest together, or close to the diagonal line. Thus, Figure 5-13B represents considerable saving over Figure 5-13A. More of the total volume is closer to the diagonal, and therefore moves a shorter total distance.

The requirement of a travel chart controls cost by insuring that any recommended change will reduce rather than increase the cost of material handling.

Flow Charts

A flow chart, Figure 5-14, is an analytical tool for revealing hidden costs of manufacture, such as delays, storages, and unnecessary transportation.[10] They are hidden because they usually do not appear on any official paper, such as an operation sheet. The flow chart has a purpose similar to that of the travel chart in that it helps to suggest ways of rearranging equipment to reduce cost.

As a control device, the flow chart has often been compared to a pawl on a ratchet wheel. It permits forward progress, changes which

[9] R. A. Olsen, *Manufacturing Management*. Scranton, Pennsylvania: International Textbook Company, 1967, Ch. 12.

[10] R. M. Barnes, *Motion and Time Study*. New York: John Wiley and Sons, 1963, p. 84.

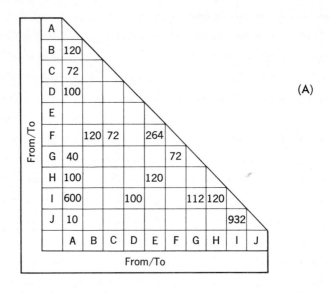

(A)

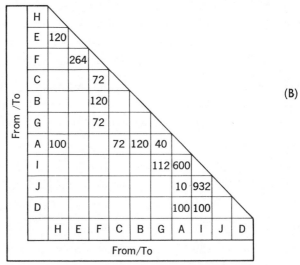

(B)

Figure 5-13A   (upper) Travel Chart before Improvement
Figure 5-13B   (lower) Travel Chart after Improvement

SOURCE: *Manufacturing Management: A Quantitive Approach* by Robert A. Olsen. International Textbook Company, Scranton, Pa.

reduce cost; but impedes backward motion, or changes which increase cost.

Organization Charts

An organization chart shows the formal relationships among members of an organization. Such charts help to clarify lines of authority and to specify areas of activity. The charts will often show which units are "line"; that is, those in direct authority and directly responsible for the primary objectives of manufacture, sales, and finance; and those which are staff, or in an advisory capacity.

Often an organization manual accompanies the chart, spelling out specific areas of authority. Together, they act as controls on the delegation of authority. In a positive sense, they indicate to each management member his relative position in the organization and the major responsibilities he is expected to fulfill. Figure 5-15A, B, C shows three typical forms of organization chart: Functional, Product, and Process.

The placement of a specific department within the organization structure often has profound implications. A quality control department reporting to the engineering or even directly to the President will exert much more control over quality than one reporting directly to a manufacturing head. The manufacturing head is usually under great pressure to "get out production." The higher the restraining voice for quality, the better chance there is for good quality. Usually, the more technical the organization, the more need there is for quality control to be independent of manufacturing.

Wage Classification Charts

A wage classification chart points out clearly to management which jobs are in line with the planned wage scale, and which ones are not. In Figure 5-16, the six jobs above the blocks have been "red-circled." This indicates they are out of line.

These exceptional conditions generally become apparent upon the installation of a job evaluation program, in which all hourly tasks are given a point value based upon the skill, effort, responsibility, and working condition requirements of the job. The objective of such a program is to help insure that the relative worth of each job is recognized in the wage rate paid.

To correct out-of-line conditions, management will attempt to:

Travel, (feet)	Symbol	Description

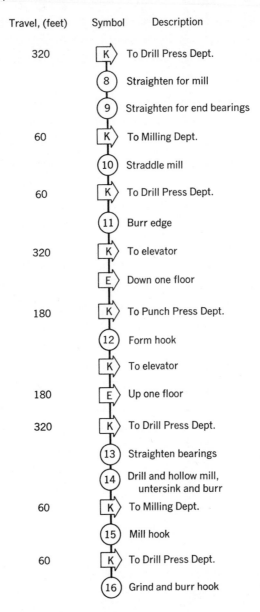

320	K	To Drill Press Dept.
	8	Straighten for mill
	9	Straighten for end bearings
60	K	To Milling Dept.
	10	Straddle mill
60	K	To Drill Press Dept.
	11	Burr edge
320	K	To elevator
	E	Down one floor
180	K	To Punch Press Dept.
	12	Form hook
	K	To elevator
180	E	Up one floor
320	K	To Drill Press Dept.
	13	Straighten bearings
	14	Drill and hollow mill, untersink and burr
60	K	To Milling Dept.
	15	Mill hook
60	K	To Drill Press Dept.
	16	Grind and burr hook

Figure 5-14 Flow Chart for Manufacture of an Armature

SOURCE: *Time and Motion Study* by R. H. Barnes. John Wiley & Sons, Inc., New York, 1963.

1. Promote the person concerned to a higher level job, with no (or a small) increase in pay;

2. Hold up or slow down annual wage increases in these "red-circle" jobs until they are in line.

Management rarely will decrease a man's pay as a result of such a determination. The damage to morale, perhaps in the entire organization, could be expected to outweigh the monetary savings of such action.

Indeed, management will first seek to determine if the job holder can be promoted to some higher-level job. This may not be feasible, due to a lack of openings or to lack of qualifications on the part of the

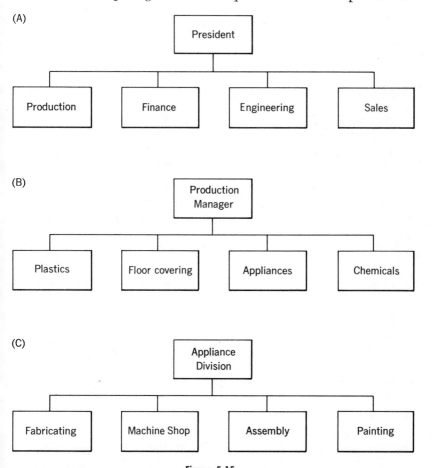

Figure 5-15
(A) Functional Organization (B) Product Organization (C) Process Organization

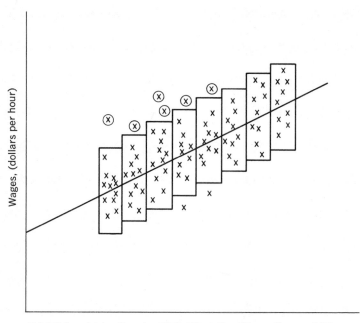

Point Value of Jobs, Based on Skill, Effort, Conditions, Responsibility

Figure 5-16   Wage Classification Chart Showing "Red Circle" Jobs

individual. Management will then determine if it is possible to hold up future raises until the job is brought in line. This may not meet with excessive resistance, particularly when no real reason exists for the wage differential. However, when a reason does exist, due to a spot shortage of that particular trade, management may be well advised to take no action at all.

In this latter case, the hope is that the higher wage will attract more aspirants for the job, and that the normal action of supply and demand will in time equalize the situation. Meanwhile, the best decision is to take no action.

The wage classification chart acts as a control by bringing to management's attention those jobs which are above or below the organization's normal salary levels. Management then may act to correct or not act to correct, as the specific exigencies of the situation may dictate.

Histograms

A mass of data on sales, production, quality, profitability, inventories, and so forth, will often be more intelligible if presented in the form of a histogram. Many kinds of data, when broken down into classes, will look something like Figure 5-17. Usually, there is a peak, and a declining order of frequency on each side of this peak. Data that can be expected to distribute in this fashion are:

1. Daily sales in a department store,
2. Clothing sales, by size, such as shoes, hats, women's dresses,
3. Dimension of manufactured work in mass production manufacture,
4. Wages paid in a large corporation,
5. Pieces produced in 8 hours by men on incentive, where no artificial ceilings exist.

Such data may be expected to follow some definite pattern whenever it is not subject to specific pressures, and can be presumed to behave randomly. These patterns are well known to statisticians, and may take the form of the Normal, Poisson, Binomial, or some other

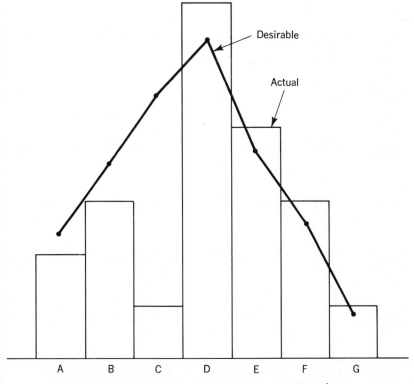

Figure 5-17 Car Unit Sales by Price Line: Histogram Example

distribution. When a specific pattern is expected, any variation from that pattern may be investigated and questioned.

Figure 5-17 represents this type of thinking. A large automobile manufacturer found himself with this pattern of sales. The line represents the desirable condition, and the block diagram or histogram represents the actual condition. The auto manufacturer can observe that his sales of cars in price category C are not doing as well as expected. He might now decide to increase his advertising, lower a particular selling price, or even produce and promote an entirely new model.

Figure 5-18 shows the amount of information that may be gleaned from histograms.[11] This example is taken from the field of quality control, but it is equally useful and applicable wherever data can be gathered, and where some concept of a specification limit is possible.

As shown, the histogram chart controls the operation by pointing out when the process is satisfactory, when it needs a simple adjustment, when the process is barely satisfactory, and other characteristics.

Again, as with other graphic controls, the chart tells the operator when to correct and when to let the process alone.

Pictorial Charts

Pictorial charts are more of an informative type of control. Facts portrayed pictorially seem to make a greater impression and last longer than facts communicated in words.

For control to exist, there must be some plan or some judgment as to direction. The "pie charts" shown in Figure 5-19 reveal that grievances due to incentives are increasing. The executive must use judgment here as to whether this increase is significant, and thus worthy of investigation. Presumably, a knowledgeable staff department would have made this determination beforehand, using some applicable statistical technique. The "pie chart" by itself does not convey the concept of significance, which is of great importance in exerting control.

The bar chart at the bottom of Figure 5-19 shows that junk, rework, and rejects are going down. This is obviously worthwhile. The

---

[11] G. B. Carson, *Production Handbook,* 2d ed. New York: Ronald Press, 1958, p. 8–23.

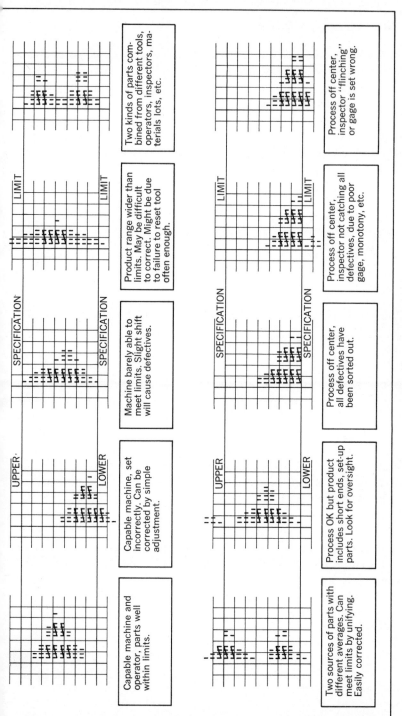

Figure 5-18 Information Possible from Histograms

SOURCE: *Production Handbook*, Second Edition, edited by Gordon B. Carson. Copyright © 1958, The Ronald Press Company, New York.

113

authors of the chart are evidently telling management that whatever action they have been taking has been worthwhile. This may be accompanied by an appeal for greater funds to continue the present course of action.

The chart presents an intuitive type of control. There is no attempt to say that the controls cost so many dollars and saved so many dollars. Reliance upon a competent staff is essential, or astute questioning is required on the part of the executive to determine the real value which the graphic control so dramatically presents.

Linear Responsibility Charts

A relatively new graphical model used for the *analysis* and *control* of organizations is the Linear Responsibility Chart.[12] This static control technique has gained widespread popularity due to its versatility, simplicity, and practicality. Figure 5-20 represents a condensed version of the responsibility chart showing position titles across the top and duties or functions at the left-hand side. The junction of the two axes shows, by various symbols, whether a person supervises, performs, influences, or has no relation to a particular task. For example, the figure indicates that the production vice president is in charge of product development, inventory control, and maintenance, while the marketing vice president is directly accountable for market research, customer service, and physical distribution. If one wished to know which positions had direct relationship with inventory control, he would read the chart horizontally and discover that the production vice president, factory supervisor, purchasing agent, and director of data processing all had some concern with the firm's inventory.

The Linear Responsibility Chart not only shows the line and staff relationships found on the traditional organization chart, but also demonstrates who performs specific tasks, who reports to whom, the size of executive workloads, and relationships among organizational elements. These charts have been effectively used to reduce overhead costs, balance workloads, identify areas of overlapping responsibility, simplify control, and increase information flow and speed of decision-making.

---

[12] "Linear Responsibility Charting: Fast Way to Clear up Confusion," *Factory,* March 1963, pp. 88–91.

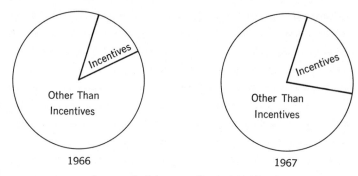

Increase in Grievances Due to Incentives
1966 Versus 1967

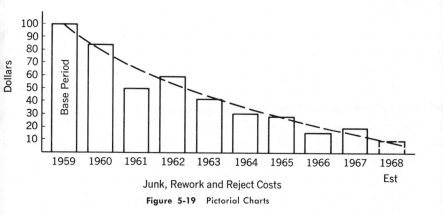

Junk, Rework and Reject Costs

Figure 5-19   Pictorial Charts

Summary

Graphic controls communicate information, facilitate decision-making, and motivate efforts toward attainment of organizational goals.

Controls may be dynamic or static. Typically, dynamic controls are Gantt, PERT, Statistical Quality Control, line and goal-seeking charts. All of these show plan versus accomplishment. Each requires periodic posting. The SQC type of chart indicates when a system is no longer behaving normally and when to investigate. The other charts depend on the judgment of the decision-maker as to whether the change is sufficiently large enough to warrant investigation and action.

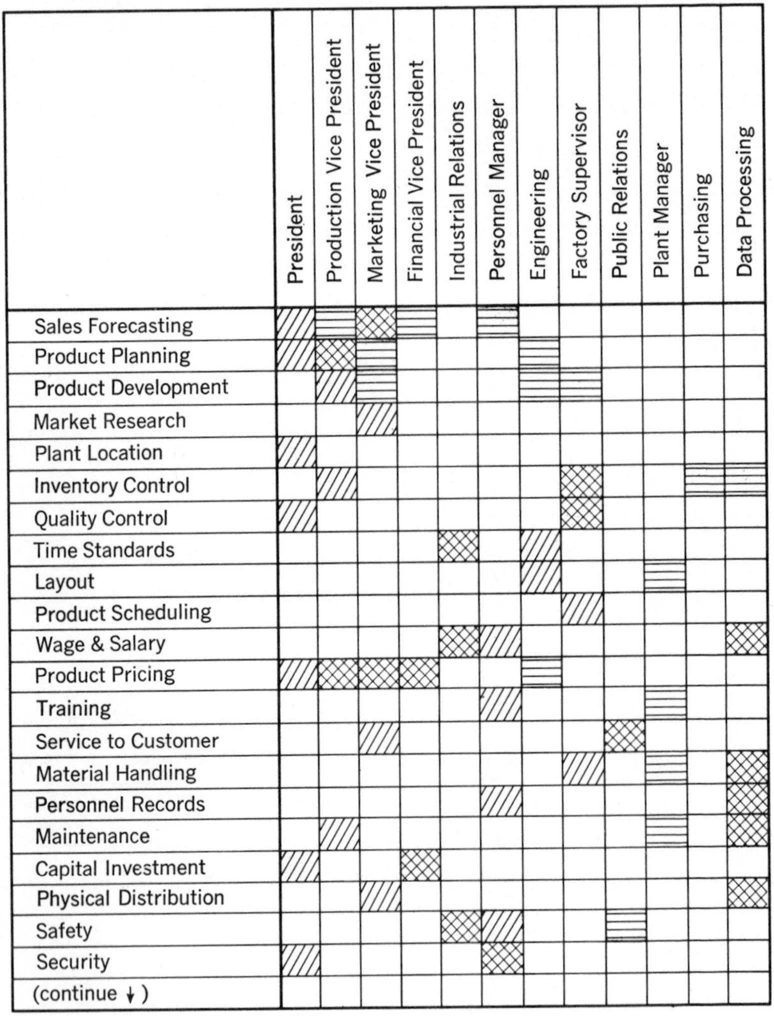

	President	Production Vice President	Marketing Vice President	Financial Vice President	Industrial Relations	Personnel Manager	Engineering	Factory Supervisor	Public Relations	Plant Manager	Purchasing	Data Processing
Sales Forecasting	/	=	X	=		=						
Product Planning	/	X	=				=					
Product Development			/	=			=					
Market Research			/									
Plant Location	/											
Inventory Control		/						X			=	
Quality Control	/							X				
Time Standards						X	/					
Layout							/			=		
Product Scheduling								/				
Wage & Salary						X	/					X
Product Pricing	/	X	X	X			=					
Training							/			=		
Service to Customer			/						X			
Material Handling								/		=		X
Personnel Records						/				=		X
Maintenance		/								=		X
Capital Investment	/			X								
Physical Distribution			/									X
Safety						X	/			=		
Security	/					X						
(continue ↓)												

Figure 5-20 Linear Responsibility Chart

Static controls may originate during the planning stage, or at the end of the process to appraise results and assist in the planning required for the next run.

Static controls originating in the planning stage include breakeven, travel, flow process, organization, wage classification, and linear responsibility charts. These controls inform those concerned of the best thinking available to date. Any change from this thinking should be challenged and subjected to the same questioning approach that was necessary before the original installation was made. When new information becomes available, the static control will help to indicate whether a change will be an improvement and thus permissible, or will not be an improvement, and thus should not be approved. Static controls, such as histograms, pie charts, bar charts, and picto-graphs are helpful in appraising results, and in determining action which should be taken in the future.

CHAPTER SIX

The Computer
and Managerial Control

A machine has not yet been built which can think like an executive, but the intelligent application of computers to managerial problems can result in more effective decision-making and control of organizational resources. This chapter provides explanations of the most important control methods made possible through electronic data processing (EDP).

Computers, and the necessary peripheral devices used in operating them, are defined as mechanical systems designed to process data at a relatively fast rate. At the present time, computers are controlled by sets of instructions (programs) developed by human beings. Machines cannot create ideas independent of the programmed instructions. Nevertheless, certain individuals do not hesitate to classify computers as intelligent, since the machines seemingly do many things which, if done by humans, would be considered as rational behavior. For example, computers can design other machines, play chess, write music, simulate the growth of cities, interpret the results of psychological examinations, and counsel students. These machines handle complex instructions and data but they have no imagination; they cannot invent and are predictable in their "behavior." The human brain has over ten billion working parts, while the most complex computer has only about one million parts; consequently, man cannot yet justify his reference to the machine as an intelligent "brain."

The quality of information generated by an electronic data processing system is directly related to the quality of data and human instructions it receives as inputs. Machines do not reason but they can process data in such a manner that results are often more objective, consistent, unbiased, and effective than those provided by a staff of humans.

Management is currently witnessing a "third generation" of computers and peripheral processing equipment. The first generation began about 1945 with the application of vacuum tubes and electro-mechanical relays in a data processing revolution, which has been compared with the Industrial Revolution in terms of its impact on society. Between 1957 and 1964 there was a growth in the application of computers to all areas of business, science, government, and education. This spread in the use of computers is called the second generation in the EDP revolution. Solid state circuits increased the capacity and reduced the size of equipment, and in 1964 there were over 18,000 operating computer systems in the United States.

In 1966, with the introduction of a series of computers which process information submitted from many remote sources, the world moved into a third generation of computer technology. This concept of shared use of computer facilities is called "time-sharing" and holds great promise for thousands of organizations which could otherwise not afford the benefits of a large computer system. As technology in telecommunications and data processing advances, more managers will have access to computers and the day may not be too distant when individual families will share the advantages of a computer utility just as they now enjoy the benefits of large telephone and electric power utilities.

Real-Time Managerial Control

Increased capabilities of electronic computers have made possible a breakthrough in the concept of managerial control. Until a few years ago, managers literally "sat upon" large amounts of valuable information because they could not retrieve it fast enough for effective use or because it was too costly to obtain in meaningful form. Recently, however, decision-making and control within diversified organizations have been facilitated by a computer model known as real-time information retrieval. This approach to managerial control implies that information is stored within the system in such a way that almost immediate access to any part of it is possible. This type of information system allows the computer to "make" decisions about real events while they are still in progress.

Real-time information systems can be contrasted with that type of system the authors choose to call "prior-time," where data are accumulated in batches over a period of time in order that they will be available at some future point in time. Most payroll systems are "prior-time" systems in that they accumulate such data as regular and overtime hours worked by each member of the force so that at one preestablished point (the end of the month) information is available to calculate and print the paychecks. It is usually not necessary for a manager to have continuous knowledge of the status of his payroll throughout the month, and, consequently, such systems are not designed for real-time operation. That is, the manager could not have immediate access to total payroll information except at the end of the established time period.

An important requirement for real-time control is "on-line" communications capability, which means that all important data sources and users within an organizational system are provided with a point of origin device connected to the central processing unit. This device is normally two-directional. It provides a communication linkage from the source of data to the central computer as well as from the central computer to the source and user of the information. In this way, information introduced at any point is immediately available for use at any other point in the system. The basic point of origin device is, in data processing language, called an input-output terminal (that is, teletypewriter or teleprinter), which is placed as near to the point of transaction as possible. For example, a real-time inventory control system would have teleprinters in all major warehouses.

The central computer of a real-time system must have certain features not required in a normal data processing system. It must be capable of establishing priorities on incoming messages, of stopping lower priority programs and placing them in storage when a message of higher priority is received, of high-speed and random-access storage, and of processing a variety of programs. These capabilities add considerably to the cost of the system. In fact, a real-time data processing network is likely to cost twice as much as a conventional computer system designed to handle the same amount of information.

Thus, it can be seen that a definite trade-off exists between speed and cost; as speed is sacrificed, the total cost of the system is reduced.

Real-Time Applications

As early as 1960, military operations were making efficient use of on-line, real-time computer systems for the control of inventories and shipments of supplies to all points of the world. For example, users of aircraft, rail, and marine supplies were connected by means of tele-typewriters to a control center in St. Louis, Missouri. When a field unit was in need of repair parts, it relayed a message to the central computer at the Materiel Command in St. Louis, which contained an updated record of the inventories existing at the four General Army Depots. If the requested parts were in stock, an order was immedi-ately sent to the nearest depot for shipment to the user. If the parts were not in stock, the computer printed a purchase order, which was sent to the purchasing department of the Materiel Command. This computer print-out contained the number of items needed, sources of supply, prices which had previously been paid, and the priority of the unit making the request.

Major airlines in this country were the first industrial organiza-tions to make widespread use of real-time information processing as a control technique. American Airlines[1] installed a real-time control system enabling the company to utilize its seating capacity more effectively and also providing better service to its customers. The con-trol system, which has been named SABRE, accumulates pertinent information related to every flight. This information is stored in a central computer which is connected by transceivers to ticket offices throughout the company's international system. The status of critical elements within the entire sphere of operation is known at any given moment. Ticket agents are strictly controlled by the computer, which is programmed to receive customer data, and, unless it receives total information pertaining to each customer, the agent is not permitted to complete his transaction.

Lockheed Aircraft[2] uses two real-time computers to continuously update production and inventory data. The Lockheed control system reports on the progress of all jobs within the plant by way of an inte-grated communications network. The data are current and any line

---

[1] "SABRE: A Thirty Million Dollar Application," *Fortune* (April 1964), pp. 142–143.

[2] "Keeping Ahead on Real-time," *Business Week*, March 27, 1965, pp. 167–170.

supervisor has immediate access to the location of materials, production schedules, rejection rate, and other information required for daily operations.

Standard Oil of New Jersey[3] uses an integrated real-time system to control its operations at a major plant. The system combines stock level control records, invoice verification, payroll and personnel operations, work schedules, shipping data, production reports, fixed asset reports, and all accounting records. Standard Oil is thus using a systems approach to operational control by relating information gathered from each element of the system in order to determine its implications on the remainder of the system.

The Pennsylvania State University[4] has demonstrated that large costs incurred during government materiel inspections can be significantly reduced through the application of a real-time control system using revised probabilities of defective material to maintain current information about suppliers. This control system is based upon the rapid gathering, integrating, and analysis of quantitative inspection information in order to develop sampling plans which minimize inspection costs for noncritical items.

This approach provides an example of how current information can be used to control operating costs. Immediate feedback regarding product quality can be transmitted to those points within the organization which have the greatest need for the data. Thus, personnel planners can determine where inspectors are needed the most. The purchasing department can be made aware of those vendors who have the poorest quality performance, and inventory control personnel will know what shipments have been rejected and the approximate delays in delivery time.

Real-time applications have not been limited to the fields of production and logistics. Westinghouse Electric Corporation has developed a sophisticated data processing system which includes a financial model permitting more effective control of the company's cash. The model maintains an up-to-the-hour account of cash flow. Receipts and expenditures of all divisions are instantaneously transmitted to the computation center where they are recorded in a centralized account. When the account at any of the Corporation's 200 regional banks falls below some predetermined level, funds are automatically shifted from

[3] R. Wasley, *Business Information and Processing Systems*. Homewood, Illinois: Richard D. Irwin, 1965.
[4] R. D. Smith, p. 254.

the central account to the regional account. Should the balance in the central account contain more reserves than required to back the regional accounts effectively, financial managers are informed and the excess funds are immediately invested in liquid assets, such as marketable securities. As a result, management is kept informed of the company's cash position on a real-time basis, and funds which previously accumulated in individual division accounts are redistributed or invested in the best interest of the Corporation as a total system.

As Martin[5] points out, the theory of real-time is to have data output from an information system immediately fed back to control current operations. In this respect, a word of caution should be given to those who anticipate real-time as the answer to all of management's problems of control. Certain managerial functions are not presently amenable to instantaneous data feedback systems. Stages of strategic planning require that top management develop ideas for subordinate staff members to study. Management must also coordinate interdepartmental approaches to the solution of problems. These functions, and many more like them, cannot be controlled by a computer.

As an example of how real-time systems might prove very impractical, consider the managerial function of performance evaluation.[6] If budgets are broken into time intervals of one month, hourly or daily information as to material and labor costs could well be wasted data, since it would not be possible to compare actual with standard costs under this condition. Also, it would likely be most expensive and ineffective to evaluate variances (if they could be detected) and attempt corrective action on such a short time basis. Affected personnel could well become immune to the significance of budgetary control.

It is not likely that the next decade will find the chief executive face to face with a computer in a cold and staffless organization where the task of control is delegated to one of electronic rather than human interaction. However, since mechanized decision-making is in an early stage of development, it is difficult to predict the long-range potential of real-time managerial systems. For the present, it is safe to say that the cost of a completely automated information-decision system outweighs its practical value.

---

[5] E. W. Martin, *Electronic Data Processing.* Homewood, Illinois: Richard D. Irwin, 1965, p. 381.

[6] John Dearden, "Myth of Real-time Management Information." *Harvard Business Review*, May–June 1966, pp. 123–132.

The Need for Real-Time

Before initiating a feasibility study to determine the practicality of installing a real-time computer control system, the manager must first answer the following questions:[7]

1. What decisions need to be made within the organization?
2. What information is needed in order to make each of these decisions?
3. Where can this information be obtained most effectively and efficiently?
4. How much time can be allowed to elapse between an event's occurrence and the response to that occurrence?
5. Is it likely that information originating from unexpected sources will bear heavily on the decisions? (If chance information does play a significant role in decision-making, such as the case with escaping refugees during time of war, it is difficult to establish preprogrammed computerized strategies.)
6. How much interaction is required between the system and the decision-maker? If significant amounts of questioning must be conducted before a decision can be reached, it will be difficult to provide the computer with sufficient rules to allow for all contingencies. Even in this area, however, technology seems to be attempting the impossible. In May 1967, CBS Television's "21st Century" demonstrated a computerized system which made initial diagnosis of medical and psychological problems based on symptoms which the patient read into the processor. After each symptom was input to the machine, the computer "responded" with additional questions in order to determine as much as possible about each symptom in much the same way as a medical doctor approaches a diagnosis.

If the answers to the above questions indicate a need for a control system operating on a real-time basis, then a fast, economical, and comprehensive communication network will almost certainly be required. This network would function most efficiently with a computer at its "nerve" center.

Organization Structure

Since organization provides the means for decision-making, an important consideration is the effect of real-time control upon a firm's organizational structure. In the early twenties, a trend toward decentralization was begun by General Motors. Since that time some firms have found centralized decision-making to their best advantage while others have successfully followed General Motors toward de-

[7] F. DePaula, "The Implications of Real-time Systems for Management Control." *The Computer Bulletin*, X (June 1966), p. 24.

centralization. The feeling is that centralized decisions are more effective, especially if management wishes to optimize from a total systems point of view. However, as the complexities of operating a large business become greater, traditional information systems become more and more inadequate, thus making it impossible to control an enterprise by means of centralized decision-making techniques.

If, however, a rapid communication network can be integrated with an information assimilation, analysis, and interpretation system, the efficiencies of centralized decision-making can be more fully realized. Such is the possibility offered by real-time data processing.[8]

Time-shared Control Systems

Advances in EDP technology have provided for more efficient utilization of computer capacity through "time-sharing," which allows many users to take advantage of the large-scale computer from remote locations. Instead of each business enterprise providing its own computer system, a group of businesses shares one large computer. No longer will the competitive organization be able to rely upon the high cost of computer systems as an excuse to ignore electronic processing of its information. The third generation computer now makes it technically and economically feasible to bring the full advantages of large-scale centralized processing units to anyone who has teletypewriter service available in his home or office.

The applications of time-sharing to managerial control are many and varied. Savings and loan associations use computers to post and validate transactions while simultaneously updating master files. Central computers in a time-shared network protect banking institutions from fraudulent transactions by providing current information about the size of accounts in branch organizations. Hotels make use of on-line computer systems to provide immediate listing of customer accounts. Previously, last minute charges were not posted to the account until the following day and these institutions were faced with many unpaid items of expense. With time-sharing, up-to-the minute statements are prepared at the press of a button. In hospitals, nurses are automatically informed of the time and type of medications prescribed for all patients in their care. Utility companies have access to current information from remote locations as to the amount

---

[8] For a further discussion on the subject of trends in organization structure and the effects of information technology on managerial control, refer to "Management in the 1980's" by H. J. Leavitt and T. L. Whisler in the *Harvard Business Review,* November–December 1958, pp. 41–48.

of power which is being generated and how much is being used. Through this time-shared technique, management can control load requirements more effectively and efficiently. Educational institutions use time-sharing to control bursar transactions and classroom allocations during registration periods when up-to-date information is critical.

This progress demands that the executive who wishes to maintain pace with his competition learn as much as and as fast as possible about the subject of time-sharing a large computer versus private ownership of a small computer. It is an accepted fact that machines are being used more and more in the control of men and other machines. Consequently, those who neglect to adapt their organization to this changing environment will find that competition has reduced its cost of control, reduced operating expenditures, and increased profits at the expense of the noncomputerized enterprise.

At the time of writing, one public computer utility is already in operation in the New England area. This utility is operated by the Keydata Corporation of Boston and provides a variety of business services to about 100 different organizations at a small fraction of the cost if the same services were provided by individually owned computers. Communications with the central computer are by teletype lines from teletypewriters and printers located at the users' work sites. The Keydata time-shared system provides such services as billing, inventory control, customer credit checking, file storage and retrieval, development of accounting reports, and the analysis of customer relationships.

Characteristics of such time-shared systems which have important implications for managerial control are summarized below:[9]

1. The interaction between the central processor and the distant user is almost instantaneous so that the user receives service almost indistinguishable from that which he would receive if he were physically present in the same room as the computer.

2. Each subscriber to a time-shared system can be provided with an indefinitely expandable and instantaneously accessible private file system which is fully protected against unauthorized access.

3. The technological achievements and data collections of many individuals and organizations can be combined in files (such as in trade associations) so that the contents are simultaneously available to all users of the systems.

---

[9] D. F. Parkhill, *The Challenge of the Computer Utility*. Reading, Massachusetts: Addison-Wesley Publishing Company, 1966, pp. 154–155.

4. Small businessmen can improve their competitive positions through access to the same sophisticated planning and control techniques, market reports, and accounting methods as their larger counterparts in the business community.

If the executive wishes to investigate the feasibility of adding computer capabilities to his organization by means of the time-sharing method, he need not be overly concerned with the matter of computer programming. The International Business Machines Corporation, for example, has recently marketed its third generation 360 Series of multiple user computers. A central processor in this series has effective storage capacity for 32 billion bits of data as compared to its previous generation, which had capacity averaging about 50,000 bits of data.

This tremendous increase in storage capacity makes it possible to maintain thousands of standard or library programs for immediate call-up by any user. Thus, the burden of programming is absorbed by the supplier of the computer service while the user is merely responsible for determining the specifications of his particular business system.[10] If, for example, a shipping department wishes to use a linear programming algorithm (model) to solve a transportation and warehousing problem, it would simply input certain costs and required amounts of materials, call for the preprogrammed Simplex Model, and wait a few seconds for an optimum shipping schedule to be calculated by the central computer.

The concept of time-sharing, at the present, appears to have its greatest potential for medium- and small-size organizations. For larger organizations, special difficulties arise when attempts are made to share large computer systems. In most large businesses, for example, computing involves great volumes of data. For such masses of figures, inexpensive peripheral (input-output) devices, such as the teletypewriter cannot be effectively used. Instead, high speed equipment must be used which often costs as much as a small computer. Also, when data are to be transmitted over long distances, the costs become much greater as the volume of work increases, making it difficult for larger organizations to justify a time-shared system.[11]

---

[10] The user must specify his inputs (documents, volumes, number of reports, time available); outputs (form, volume, frequency); important files (size and content); flow charts showing the objectives desired; and special problems which arise on an infrequent basis.

[11] F. C. Withington, *The Use of Computers in Business Organizations.* Reading, Massachusetts: Addison-Wesley Publishing Company, 1966, pp. 103–104.

Simulation as a Technique for Managerial Control

One of the most powerful managerial control devices provided by operations research personnel in recent years is that of simulation. Simulation is a relatively simple technique whereby a model is built which represents a real-world system or subsystem. The model is then manipulated in an attempt to improve the real situation which it represents.

Models of various types have long been used for training purposes. Maps serve as descriptive models to teach students the relative location of parts of the earth's surface. The Link Trainer is used to simulate the operations of an aircraft so that the student pilot can practice takeoff and landing maneuvers without leaving the ground. Large mock-ups are used to simulate space travel. And most of us are familiar with the mathematical model which states that the square of the hypotenuse of a right triangle is equal to the sum of the squares of the other two sides. All of these seemingly unrelated models have something in common—each represents some aspect of a real situation.

Besides *training*, however, models have another very useful purpose; that of *improving* the actual situation. Model railroads are used to plan more efficient switching operations, three-dimensional models are used to develop effective plant layouts, and the Rand Corporation has designed a simulation model for improving our defense against potential attack from the air.[12]

Operations research specialists and industrial engineers have provided many useful analytical tools which can be applied to managerial control problems. For example, linear programming models have been useful in solving product mix and allocation of resources problems; queueing models have been useful in certain cases where employees are required to stand in line waiting for tools or where customers form waiting lines in front of bank windows. The Theory of Games has application to competitive situations where two strategists are involved. While these tools have had practical applications, they very often cannot be used because the decision problems just do not fit the assumptions (constraints) which are inherent in the various models.

When problems do become so complex that proven analytical

---

[12] Elias H. Porter, *Manpower Development*. New York: Harper & Row, Publishers, 1964.

models cannot be used in their solution, or when it becomes dangerous to "make the problem fit the model," a much more flexible approach is possible. This alternative method of solving problems is called *simulation,* a technique whereby a model is designed which represents the control problem facing the executive. Such models help to clarify the problem, assist in predicting the behavior of a part of a business operation when certain changes occur, and they even suggest decisions which can be made to benefit the organization.

A manager can simulate a complete year of his operation in a matter of minutes or, if he prefers, he can slow down the operation so that he can analyze just what is happening in his problem areas— a process analogous to slow motion or "instant replay." Thus, the manager for the first time has a laboratory in which he can study his resources and view their interactions either in slow motion or at high speed. The manager, through system simulation, can improve his ability to forecast and control. He can observe before he acts, and can test ideas and changes before implementing them. The results of several alternatives can be determined in a matter of seconds if so desired.

Thus far, the discussion of simulation has been quite general. Perhaps a practical example will aid the reader by demonstrating the real value of this technique to the managerial control function.

A simple EOQ (Economic Order Quantity)[13] formula exists which yields the size of an order that should be placed to minimize total inventory costs (carrying cost and order cost). In order to use this model, it is assumed that demand is known in advance, that it will remain constant, and that the interval between the time an order is placed and the time it is received for inventory (lead time) is also constant. If these assumptions can be made, then it is possible to apply the formula which will yield the "exact" quantity that should be ordered to minimize the total inventory cost.

However, it is common knowledge that very few situations in the real business world lend themselves to this form of analysis. Demand usually varies from day to day and suppliers are seldom capable of providing certain delivery dates.

---

[13] $\text{EOQ} = \left(\dfrac{2RS}{CI}\right)^{\frac{1}{2}}$ where R = yearly demand, S = the cost of placing an order, C = the cost of one item, and I = percentage allowance for carrying the item in inventory for one year.

Simulation helps to provide better control decisions even in the face of uncertainty. From past history of occurrence of events (demand and lead time) further history can be generated or "simulated" and observations can be made regarding the results of various strategies which the executive may wish to try. For example, what would be the effect of changing the ordering policy from "Order 100 skins of a particular type of leather every time the stock level falls to five skins" to "Order 50 skins each time the inventory falls to 10"?

A shoe manufacturer may have historical information showing that demand has never exceeded 15 nor been less than 7 skins per day and that the probability of 7 skins being demanded on any day is 0.05; of 8 skins, 0.10; of 9 skins, 0.15; and so forth, up to the probability of 0.05 for 15 skins. The manufacturer also knows that the time it takes to receive an order varies between one and three days and the probability of one-day delivery is 0.40, of two-day delivery, 0.40, and of three-day delivery, 0.20. This means that during the past, two out of every five orders were received in one day, two out of every five orders were received in two days, and one order in every five took three days for delivery.

With this information, management can simulate numerous days of experience to determine the impact of various possible ordering rules upon such variables as inventory levels, number of orders placed, the sales which would be lost because no inventory was available, and the total cost of inventory. Using a technique commonly referred to as Monte Carlo, a model can be built which simulates the real world inventory problem, or any of a magnitude of managerial control problems. This so-called Monte Carlo method permits an executive to experiment with many hypothetical decision alternatives without disrupting real world conditions. In other words, one can experiment on paper or with the computer subsequent to actually using the most favorable alternative in the operation of a business. The computer, in a sense, provides a managerial control laboratory for experimental decision making.

The essence of this type of simulation lies in utilizing past history to predict future events through the Monte Carlo method. An examination of how this tool is applied follows. In the example given above, lead time for delivery could be only one of three values: one, two, or three days. Each value had a specific probability of occurrence based on what had happened in the past. What is needed is some type of random number generator which would yield the same proportion of delivery times as existed in the real world. That is, if someone were to select numbers from a list, 40 out of every 100 should represent a delivery time of one day; 40 of the 100 should represent two days; and the remaining 20 numbers represent three days. Such lists of numbers do exist and are called Random Number Tables, which contain columns of randomized digits. If one enters the table at the top of a column and selects consecutive digits, it can be assumed that the selections will be random. Now that the Monte Carlo method has been described, a return is made to the lead time problem and the following chart is established:

Random Number	Lead Time in Days
00–39	1
40–79	2
80–99	3

Then, if the first number selected from the table is 73, it is representative of a lead time of two days, since it falls within the interval between 40 and 79. A number 98 represents a three-day lead time and the number 17 represents one-day delivery. When this experiment is performed over and over again, the law of large numbers provides reasonable certainty that 40 out of every 100 selections will yield a lead time of one day; 40 out of every 100 will yield a two-day delivery time; and 20 out of 100, a three-day lead time. This is exactly what took place in the real world before the simulation model was designed.

Following the same procedure for simulating demand, one can match the lead time event with the demand event over hundreds or even thousands of days of experience to see what effect various decisions will have on inventory costs. The computer makes this possible, since a random-number generator is stored on its memory drum and the machine is programmed to run many alternative decisions in a few seconds and to provide the manager with that alternative yielding the lowest cost.

Select the rule that orders 50 skins each time the inventory level reaches 10. What the model will do is simulate demand as well as lead time each time an order has to be placed over an extended period of hypothetical operations. It will compute the cost of carrying the skins in stock, the cost of lost sales which result from being out of stock, as well as the cost of each order which has to be placed. But the trick is that the computer can do these calculations so fast that it can yield several years of data in a few seconds. Thus, the manager can try the rule of ordering 20 skins each time inventory falls to 5, or ordering 25 each time inventory falls to 10, and so forth, until he finds the combination which yields the lowest inventory cost. Before computers were invented, such a procedure would be considered ridiculous, since it would cost more to perform the calculations than could ever be saved through lower inventory costs.

Simulation allows a manager to experiment with a model to learn more about a real-world situation which he is attempting to control. Simulations can be useful in studying many types of problems previously "resolved" by intuition. As another example, consider the personnel manager's decision regarding the allocation of his recruiting resources. He has a certain amount of funds available and has several methods of applying them (college campus interviews, newspaper advertising, local interviews, company visits, and journal advertising). If he has some information about the probabilities of obtaining and retaining successful employees through each of these methods, the manager will be able to apply a simulation model to aid in his allocation decision. In other words, he can vary the amounts spent in each area in order to determine the effects of each decision upon his total recruiting program.

If simulation is to serve as an effective control technique, extreme caution must be exercised in the development of the model to assure that critical relationships among variables are not overlooked or oversimplified. This danger can be lessened when top management participates in the design of the model, when all managers who are expected to use the results are involved in the development of information inputs, and are in full understanding of the results and the manner in which the results are derived and used.

Radio Corporation of America is currently developing a long-range financial planning model including most of the significant variables related to the liquidity, profitability, and turnover activities of the firm. The simulation model includes the most probable, the pessimistic, and the optimistic estimates of such key variables as demand, material costs, and manpower requirements and is sensitive to variations in external economic conditions. It is hoped that this model will permit operating executives within each of the firm's 20 divisions, through the use of video display terminals in their offices, to make hypothetical changes in financial strategy and immediately determine the effects of their decisions on the profitability of the total system.

The Office of Naval Research is supporting several projects dealing with the construction of simulation models which can be used for managerial control purposes. Researchers working for the Navy on such studies are particularly interested in those executive functions which involve well-defined systems where inputs are to be transformed by human and capital resources into desired outputs. Examples of such systems are oil refineries, steel mills, hospitals, and data processing centers. These researchers look upon the manager as a monitor who observes and reacts to information which indicates the state of the system at any point in time. They assume that the manager can improve his understanding of information and his ability to control changes in the system by experimenting with the significant variables which interact within the system. They feel that a manager's past experience can be advantageously used to control future deviations through use of a simulation model.[14]

The preceding paragraph emphasizes the importance of theory in the development of workable management tools. The Federal Government has been responsible for vast amounts of theoretical studies in management techniques which have, in turn, resulted in useful models, such as PERT, discussed in an earlier chapter. Most of the basic research in data processing was sponsored through federal grants to IBM and Remington Rand during World War II. The point is that scientific experimentation has provided the basis for the managerial control devices discussed in this chapter; consequently, when concepts, such as simulation, are presented, the reader should have every confidence that these concepts have been carefully developed, tested, and applied to the resolvement of managerial problems.

In one of the Navy studies,[15] researchers built a simulation model of a computer center and asked the manager of that center to utilize the model as an integral part of his control process. In using the model, the following steps were followed:

1. Certain alternative courses of action were simulated.
2. Based upon the simulation data, the alternative which the manager felt to be most appropriate was selected.

---

[14] James L. McKenny, *Simulation for Control*. Western Management Science Institute, Working Paper No. 91, December 1965.

[15] McKenny, p. 2.

3. The manager implemented, in reality, the alternative course of action which he selected.

4. Researchers observed and recorded the results of the action.

The purposes in developing the model were: to determine if it could help the manager in his control function, and to reduce the cost of computer service and the time it takes to provide that service to the users.

Building the simulation model required the gathering of specific data regarding the number and type of data processing jobs processed in a given time period, the length of queue (number of jobs waiting to be processed), the amount of time the main computer was being utilized, total processing time, and the total time a job remained in the system from the time a customer turned it in until it was ready to be picked up. Once these data were determined for an extended period of history, a simulation model was developed.

After the manager of the computer center was shown that the simulation model closely represented his actual operation, he found it very useful in testing various decisions before implementing them; he was able to test different batching alternatives to determine which would most likely be processed the fastest; and he was able to determine the influence of nonscheduled express runs on his normal system.

The simulation model developed and tested for this particular Navy study introduced two new decision rules for managerial control. One rule prohibited batching more than six jobs in the morning and the other instructed the operator to use all of a particular piece of processing equipment (IBM 1401) on output when a queue of input tapes built up before the main computer.[16]

The far-reaching control possibilities of simulation have not been limited to military and business applications. At the present time, an interesting project is being conducted at the University of Southern California dealing with the simulation of an entire city. The objective of the research is to develop a computerized management program for the city of South Gate, California, which has a population of approximately 60,000, while at the same time working on a general-purpose simulation model which would be applicable to any city with a population between 30,000 and 300,000. The model includes such elements as a master zoning plan, schedule for police patrols, location of new fire stations, and optimum distribution of firefighting

---

[16] McKenny, p. 8.

equipment among existing facilities, traffic control patterns, and scientific planning of school, park, and playground facilities.

The reader who desires a more complete coverage of the subject of simulation, which includes examples of how to apply simulation to problems of control, may refer to *Management Decision Making*,[17] which provides good coverage of this subject.

To summarize the Monte Carlo approach to managerial control, consider the following:

1. Simulation allows the manager to experiment with a system without interfering with the real world situation.

2. From past history and frequency of occurrence of events, further history is generated so that the manager can observe what will happen when parameters of the system are altered.

3. Several years of history can be generated in a few seconds so that the manager can afford to perform many experiments at relatively low cost without having to wait months or years to discover the outcome of decisions and without running the risk of endangering the stability of the organization.

Business Games

Models of a broader scale have been developed to simulate entire segments of a business system. These models are called business games and are used extensively in management development programs and university classes to provide managers and students of management with greater insight and skills in dealing with managerial problems. In a business simulation game, the participant assumes the role of a manager and is required to make critical operating decisions based on information provided about the company and general business environment. Data are provided on past operations and the simulation manager is asked to make decisions about the future based on these data. The decisions are fed to a computer, which has been preprogrammed to react according to the type of decision inputs supplied by the hypothetical managers. The output from the computer provides the results of the decision in the form of production efficiency, increased sales, or market value of the firm's stock depending upon the type of game being played.

In a business simulation game (MARKSIM) developed at The Pennsylvania State University, a marketing manager is faced with

---

[17] Max D. Richards and Paul S. Greenlaw, *Management Decision Making*. Homewood, Illinois: Richard D. Irwin, 1966, pp. 498–524.

decisions, such as setting prices and determining advertising outlays. The student of management is given the opportunity to apply such fundamental concepts as price elasticity, marginal cost analyses, economic order quantity, and break-even analysis. Operating decisions must be made regarding national advertising, advertising allowances to retailers, quality, price, amount to be produced, and the number of units to be shipped to various distribution centers. In addition, the decision-maker can purchase such marketing research information as the amount of advertising used by competitors, potential sales, market potentials for coming years, and the company's present share of the market. The computer evaluates the effects of these decisions in a simulated economy and provides a convenient tool for testing new business strategies as well as for training executives.

Simulation of Cognitive Processes

Most conventional business applications of computers fall into one of the following categories: billing, inventory accounting, financial accounting, and production control. However, another type of application is receiving noteworthy attention—the simulation of human cognitive processes. A computer model has been developed which simulates the thought processes of a psychologist as he interprets psychological test results used in the selection and placement of personnel.[18] Given certain job requirements (numerical ability, sociability, clerical aptitude, responsibility), psychological test scores, and personal attributes, a psychologist is able to predict whether or not a person will likely be successful in a particular position.

Analysis of the decision processes used by the psychologist in performing this interpretation enabled researchers to build a model which yielded virtually the same results as the human analyst at about one-tenth of the cost. Other simulation models have been developed which can select stocks for a portfolio given certain investment objectives, locate warehouses, and so forth.

Management Information Systems

If information is to be accepted as the essential element of control, management must be interested in developing an information

---

[18] Robert D. Smith and Paul S. Greenlaw, "Simulation of a Psychological Decision Process." *Management Science,* April 1967, pp. 409–419.

system which will provide relevant facts as fast as possible to all personnel in the organization who need them. Computer technology has provided a good method for accomplishing these feats.

The method is called "information retrieval" and, although a computer is not absolutely necessary for a functioning retrieval system, it does much to facilitate the process. An acceptable definition of an information retrieval system is "a set of procedures for storing items in a file in an organized way, so that they can be found in the future by people who are interested." [19] This definition fits even the most antiquated filing system where a secretary might "hide" correspondence alphabetically according to the first letter of the first word on each page. It is a certainty that most executives reading this chapter have, during the absence of their secretary, spent harried moments attempting to retrieve an important piece of correspondence. Would it not be ideal if, by pushing a set of buttons, one could flash a microfilm copy of important correspondence or financial reports on a viewer built into the top of a desk? This type of retrieval system is presently on the market but, as yet, it is not priced at a level which would permit widespread adoption.

There are various information retrieval systems which are fully developed and in use. One of the first of these to be made operative was called the Selective Dissemination of Information System. Operating managers found it was almost impossible to keep up with significant literature that was related to their fields of specialization. Consequently, each of the executives of the firm was assigned a journal, the articles in which he was required to abstract. The abstracts were identified by key words, such as: Systems Analysis, Communications, PERT, Financial Audit, and Computer Language. Also, each executive was asked to develop a set of key words applicable to his particular areas of job interest. The lists and the abstracts were coded and key-punched in such a manner that each participant of the retrieval system received a hard-copy print-out of all abstracted articles containing key words which the participant had identified. Of course, this type of retrieval system is very expensive when attempted on an independent or in-house basis. However, the cost of the information could be greatly reduced by purchasing the services of an outside supplier who specialized in providing key-coded abstracts to a number of subscribers. For example, an industrial

---

[19] J. Dearden and F. McFarlan, *Management Information Systems.* Homewood, Illinois: Richard D. Irwin, 1966, p. 114.

relations manager would certainly be interested in reading abstracts of current articles key-coded under the titles, collective bargaining, wage and salary, contract negotiations, and arbitration. For a few dollars a month, executives could have access to the latest literature in their fields with the opportunity to obtain reprints of those articles of critical relevance. The School of Business at the University of Wisconsin is currently supplying this type of information to its faculty.

The Systems Development Corporation of California[20] has designed a salary information retrieval system using the concept of computer time-sharing. Participating companies supply data regarding their salary structure, job classifications, and other compensation factors. A highly classified data base is then built from these inputs. The companies receive periodic reports stating salary averages by job classification for their own firm, as well as complete classification information for all other companies with which they have exchange agreements.

By manipulating data contained in the base, member organizations can determine the effects of salary increases on their overall compensation system and budget requirements without actually effecting any changes in their everyday operations. The firms can also determine how various salary strategies compare with those already in use by other firms in the industry. Users can obtain standardized descriptions for new jobs from the data base or determine how their own descriptions compare with those used by other companies. Because the system is time-shared, large amounts of information are available at a small percentage of the cost of maintaining similar files and data processing facilities on an individual basis.

Certain organizations are currently experimenting with integrated information systems whereby selection and performance evaluation models are combined to form closed-loop control over decision processes. For example, managerial performance is measured and evaluated and future recruiting strategies are formulated to maximize the probability of obtaining potentially effective managerial personnel based on the appraisal information.

Indexing and abstracting of information are the two major problems associated with the development of low cost retrieval systems.

---

[20] *Systems Development Corporation Magazine,* vol. 9, no. 11, November 1966, pp. 11–12.

Heavy research is being conducted in these problem areas and within a few years such systems should be available on a national basis. As optical scanners, which can "read" directly from a printed page to a computer memory, are perfected, the advantages of information retrieval systems will become more valuable to the managerial control function.

Currently, modern information retrieval techniques are more often applied to the medical, legal, and education professions and not yet vital to successful business operations. The following are areas within business organizations where information retrieval systems have been found most useful to date.

1. Personnel records and skill profiles, which enable managers to evaluate personnel performance immediately; perform statistical analyses of labor usage, requirements, and costs; as well as to locate instantly those personnel within the organization who could bring special skills to bear on nonroutine problems.

2. Storage of engineering drawings and change orders.

3. Financial and operating data.

4. Technical research library.

5. Union and arbitration information.

6. Market research information.

In order that management make optimum use of available knowledge for control of the organization, a proposed management information system should be established which accomplishes the following:

1. It acquires internal as well as external information.

2. Only that information which is relevant is selected and insignificant or marginal information is rejected at an early stage of the retrieval process.

3. The system provides for selective recall of information through accurate indexing methods.

4. Summaries of critical articles and books should be stored in the form of abstracts for convenient reference.

5. The system maintains a current listing of the professional interests of its users—it continuously matches newly received information against these interest profiles and disseminates knowledge accordingly.

6. It stores information for future retrieval in such a manner as to allow for immediate and random access.

7. It provides a master file of its contained knowledge.

8. It allows for duplicate storage of critical records.

9. Classified documents must be well secured and only accessible to qualified users on a need-to-know basis.

10. Information is stored in such a way as to be exchanged easily with organizations having related interests.

11. A user feedback system is provided to adjust profiles and improve service.[21]

In conclusion, a management information system involves the following elements:

Data gathering and storage   Operation guidance (direction)
Data analysis   Reporting (feedback)
Decision-making

Today's management information system, in integrated form, consists of two major elements: information handling and managerial decision-making.[22] Since no company can afford to develop an information system for each manager, a systems analysis must be made to determine which group of managers should be included in each information network. The objective should be to keep the group as small as possible while still achieving an adequate return on investment.

Heuristic Approach to Information Control

In many decision situations there is so much information available that the executive is not able to discern which is significant and which is trivia. For example, a particular battery of psychological tests used in the selection of clerical personnel contains twenty scores, some of which are pertinent to particular types of positions while others are not. If the test evaluator were not able to distinguish between which information was relevant and which was not, his decision-making capability would be seriously limited. Consequently, it is necessary to control the flow of information when seeking solutions to complex problems. Heuristics provide such a method of control by limiting the amount of search the decision-maker must use in order to achieve a workable solution to his problem.

---

[21] J. F. Manning, "Relating a Retrieval Program to Your Company Needs." *Proceedings of the International Management Congress*, 1963, p. 256.

[22] A. H. Winchell, "Mechanizing Information Systems." *Automation*, October 1965, pp. 64–68.

Until recent years, the word heuristic was seldom found in literature pertaining to the field of management. However, the revolution in modern decision theory has brought with it a change in terminology and concept. Terms such as artificial intelligence ("teaching" a computer to solve complex problems) and heuristic programming have taken on special significance as management becomes more scientific.

"Heuristic" is defined by Webster as "serving to discover or reveal" but more precise etymological analysis shows that heuristic is taken from the Greek "heureka," supposedly made famous by Archimedes as he accidentally discovered his law of buoyancy. A literal definition of heureka would find Archimedes less than an accurate linguist, for, strictly speaking, the word implies a finding made after a planned search. Thus, the English heuristic adapted from heureka means something that assists in the reduction of search.

While a heuristic is something that contributes to the reduction of search in problem-solving activity, a heuristic program is a type of model usually amenable to mechanization on a digital computer. More specifically, a heuristic program has been defined as a "detailed prescription or strategy that *controls* the *sequences* of responses of a system to a complex task.[23] It should be pointed out that heuristic solutions to problems are not necessarily the best or optimum solutions, since many alternatives are often excluded from consideration which are hopefully irrelevant but, in fact, may not be. Heuristic problem solvers, however, in their attempts to control the amount and significance of available information, turn their approach from a search for the optimum answer to one that, with high probability, is suitable for their purposes.

Heuristic procedures can be applied when a decision situation consists of such a wide variety of alternatives that complete listing and evaluation would either be impossible or impractical. In other cases, heuristics (rules of thumb) make it possible to group large classes of strategies under a single heading which can be evaluated in itself rather than considering each of its elements individually. Heuristics can also be developed which facilitate the selection of a desired alternative by means of sequential instructions of the DO, IF, and GO TO types. For example, a heuristic decision rule might be stated as follows: "IF the applicant's mental ability score is

---

[23] Herbert Simon, *The New Science of Management Decision.* New York: Harper & Row, 1960, p. 6.

below 40, GO TO the clerical ability score. IF this score is below 25, reject applicant." By considering only two variables of a possible twenty test scores, it becomes possible to screen a large number of applicants from further consideration, thus reducing the number of alternatives relevant to the final selection decision.

Still another application of heuristics requires that the decision-maker fractionate or subdivide a complex problem into separate components. The objective then becomes one of finding a solution to each of the components, with the ultimate hope that these individual solutions, when combined, will provide a solution to the overall problem. This technique is sometimes used in the analysis of complex systems. For example, each of the subsystems of quality control, maintenance, inventory control, and scheduling might be analyzed independently in terms of their individual inputs and outputs before attempting to design a more efficient production system.

Since the application of heuristics to the control of decision-making has been made almost entirely in conjunction with data processing equipment, many persons have erroneously assumed that computational speed has been used to replace logic and selectivity in heuristic decision-making. Newell assailed this viewpoint by citing the fact that problem-solving, whether by man or machine, implies selection and control rather than mere rapid behavior, and that a true heuristic program is developed in such a way as to replicate organized behavior of sound logicians.[24]

Heuristic problem-solving techniques are best applied to ill-structured and complex situations where variables are difficult to define precisely and mathematical models are not available for their solution. Heuristics provide an objective approach to unstructured problems since they help to make experience and judgment explicit and, by so doing, systematize the selection processes used by the human decision-maker.

In order to apply heuristic methods to the control of information and eventual resolution of complex problems, Stanford Optner suggests that the following steps be taken:

1. A chart should be made of the problem process showing each point where a principal decision is made.
2. Details of the principal decision process steps must be described.

[24] A. Newell, H. Simon, and J. Shaw, "The Processes of Creative Thinking" in *Contemporary Approaches to Creative Thinking*, Edited by Gruber, Terell, and Wertheimer. New York: Atherton Press, 1962, pp. 161–167.

3. The principal alternatives and how they were generated must be demonstrated.
4. The assumptions pertinent to each alternative must be identified.
5. The criteria by which each alternative will be judged must be fully stated.
6. Detailed presentation of data, data relationships, and the procedural steps by which data were evaluated must be part of the solution.
7. The major alternative solutions, and details to explain why other solutions were eliminated must be given.[25]

In order to provide deeper insight and perhaps better understanding of the preceding paragraphs regarding heuristic control of information, selected applications of this technique are given below.

Warehouse Location.[26] The authors of this program defined their problem as one of determining a more profitable geographical pattern of warehouse locations through equating the marginal cost of operating an additional warehouse with the transportation cost saved and the change in profits resulting from more rapid delivery. The program was subdivided into two parts. The first was used to locate warehouses one at a time until no more could be added without increasing shipping costs. The second, which the authors referred to as a "bump and shift" routine, increased the efficiency of already existing locations. Three principal heuristics were used in the first program:

1. "Most geographical locations are not good sites for regional warehouses; good locations are at or near demand concentrations."
2. "Near optimum warehouse systems can be developed by locating them one at a time, adding at each stage that warehouse which produces the greatest cost savings for the entire system."
3. "Only a small subset of all possible warehouse locations need to be evaluated in detail at each stage of the analysis to determine the next warehouse site which should be added."

Using the above "rules of thumb" or heuristics, the authors were able to control the amount of information which they needed to consider in order to reach a solution to their problem. The bump and shift routine was then brought in to modify solutions reached in the main program by:

---

[25] Stanford Optner, *Systems Analysis for Business and Industrial Problem-Solving.* Englewood Cliffs, New Jersey: Prentice-Hall, Inc., 1965, pp. 20 ff.
[26] A. Kuehn, and M. Hamburger, "A Heuristic Program for Locating Warehouses." *Management Science*, 9 (July 1963), pp. 643–666.

1. Eliminating any warehouse no longer economical because an added warehouse serviced most of its customers, and

2. Shifting added warehouses within their territories to determine if more economical sites could be located.

Selection of Profitable Products.[27] This heuristic application demonstrates that the overall new product marketing problem can be reduced to a series of simpler problems and, through the use of heuristic methods, a higher probability can be attached to the success of a product that is marketed for the first time. The major problem is divided into three subproblems. The first subproblem is concerned with the rating of such variables as growth potential, seasonal fluctuation, and durability; the second and third, while related to the first, are separated for better evaluation and consist of short- and long-range profitability measures. Indices are assigned to each subproblem and combined in the final analysis to give an overall rating to the proposed new products. In this instance a complex problem is broken into its component parts in order to make it easier for the decision-maker to objectively control and evaluate the information which is available to him.

Traveling Salesman Problem.[28] In this application of heuristics, the objective is to minimize the total amount of travel required to visit a predetermined set of clients. Combinations of cities are used by first choosing two at random and then inserting others from a list so that they add least to the length of a partially-completed sales itinerary. The total planning problem is broken into separate territories and each is solved individually, after which a synthesis of the territories is completed to yield a final sales planning schedule.

Heuristic Process for the Identification of Maladjustment.[29] In this application, a computer program in current use at the Mayo Clinic identifies abnormal symptoms in patients on the basis of scores obtained on the Minnesota Multi-phasic Personality Inventory (MMPI). The original decision model dealt with the interpretation of profile patterns of MMPI maladjusted and adjusted college students. A set of decision rules was developed by taking the verbalized decision rules used by an expert test interpreter and writing a com-

---

[27] John T. O'Meara, "Selecting Profitable Products" in *Readings in Marketing*, edited by P. M. Holmes. Columbus, Ohio: Merrill, Inc., 1963, p. 314.

[28] R. Karg and G. Thompson, "A Heuristic Approach to Solving the Traveling Salesman Problem," *Management Science*, 10 (January 1964), pp. 225–248.

[29] Benjamin Kleinmuntz, "Profile Analysis Revisited: A Heuristic Approach," *Journal of Counseling Psychology*, 10, 1963, pp. 315–324.

puter program based on these decision rules. The programmed rules were then improved upon by a process of trial and error and yielded a greater percentage of accurate evaluations of maladjusted and adjusted students than did the original interpreter. Human interpretation of the MMPI takes from five to twenty minutes. This time is reduced to ten seconds on the computer and the accuracy of end results was improved by adopting the heuristic approach to problem-solving described in this section.

Controlling Computer Costs

There are four basic ways of obtaining the use of a computer. The first is through purchase. Only a small minority of users, however, buy a computer outright. Estimates are that approxmately 20 percent of present users actually own the hardware. It is not likely that a purchase would be profitable unless the prospective user were confident that he would be able to use the machine for at least five years, since average payback (lease charges versus purchase cost) is something between four and five years. It is important that the executive consider the cost of purchase as well as the fact that advances in technology are so great that a machine he buys today could well be obsolete in less than a year. Also, a purchaser often loses the advantage of free service from the computer manufacturer when he buys the equipment.

A second approach, and currently the most common method of obtaining on-site use of data processing capabilities, is through leasing. At least 80 percent of all computer users initially lease their equipment, and most of them continue to do so because of the uncertainty about obsolescence and the requirements of future application, not to mention resale value.[30]

The usual agreement requires that the customer pay a fixed charge each month based upon the nature of the basic computer and the amount of peripheral equipment (card punch, paper-tape punch, printer, card or paper-tape reader, disc files, drum files, sorter, etc.) required. Some manufacturers charge a basic fee for one shift of operation and a relatively smaller percentage figure for all hours used above the regular monthly shift. The normal leasing period runs for one year, after which the user can return the equipment with no penalty. Purchase options are granted by most manu-

---

[30] Withington, p. 36.

facturers in the event a system works well and the user feels it would be more profitable in the long run to purchase the equipment after a trial period during which rent is paid.

A third method of obtaining the use of data processing equipment is through a specialized consulting organization which sells computer service on an "as needed" basis. This form of arrangement has been especially favorable for small business firms who cannot justify the use of a computer on a full-time basis.

Another method of obtaining the benefit of high-speed information processing is through the use of the time-shared system whereby many users have remote access to a central processing computer. This concept seems to be gaining in importance with advances in microelectronic technology, especially in the area of integrated, solid state circuits, which make large volume, internal storage feasible. In fact, the new generation of computers with its large-volume, random-access memory capabilities (Control Data Corporation 6600, General Electric 645, and International Business Machines 360 Systems) has already made time-sharing a reality.

The preceding paragraphs provide general guidelines regarding the control of computer acquisition costs. The following information is relevant to the control of computer usage costs. Every effort should be made to keep data processing costs at a minimum since they can soon represent a sizable percentage of total administrative expense if not properly controlled.

For example, an executive responsible for data processing should make maximum use of the free administrative and technical assistance provided by the manufacturer. This assistance includes training courses, printed materials, programming consultants, compiler programs, and general purpose or library programs.

Since most data processing systems still use the punched card as normal input to the computer, it is wise for the executive to have an idea of what the average cost should be to have each card punched. By comparing his own costs with the standard, he will be able to better control his operating expenses. If key-punch machines are used, a total cost of two cents per card can be used as an average. This includes both the rental cost of a key-punch machine and the cost of the operator.[31]

Costs associated with the transition from older data-handling methods to computerized information processing can naturally be

---

[31] Withington, p. 41.

better controlled if they are anticipated and programmed in advance. The most important of these costs are:

1. Total systems analyses.
2. Retraining of old personnel and hiring of new personnel.
3. Rearrangement of physical facilities (improvement in air conditioning, addition of special power lines, raising of floors to provide for the lines, alteration of office space).
4. Preparation of company information for the computer to include updating and consolidation of files.
5. Parallel operations (old system is maintained until the new system has proved its reliability).

Many firms have been able to minimize the cost of switching to an advanced data-processing system through utilization of the PERT method, described in Chapter Five.

Organization Control of Data Processing

Computers are used to assist the manager in control of his everyday operations. This does not mean that he can neglect internal controls which he places over the automatic system. A computer does not make random errors of its own accord but the men who operate it are quite prone to lapses in "perfection." A computer is honest but, unfortunately, some men are inclined to stretch a few figures every now and then! Consequently, from an auditing standpoint, it has been necessary to maintain a degree of independence between the operating and accounting departments of a firm. With a data-processing system, one person often has access to a master file which stores complete transactions from purchase request to invoice transmission, thus providing the opportunity for "imaginary" transactions followed by real payments to an employee's private account. In order to preclude the possibility of internal theft, each organization using an EDP system should have a data control group and an internal auditing section, neither of which report to the director of computer operations.[32]

Summary

In order that a proposed computer system serve as an efficient and effective means of managerial control, the following general requirements should be met by the organization.

---

[32] Withington, pp. 140–142.

Top management must be knowledgeable of the capabilities and limitation of various types of computer systems. They must actively participate in the development of the particular system proposed for their organization, a system which best fits their needs and capital resources. Management must show its entire organization that it supports the computer operations.

When the organization is contemplating the installation of an electronic data processing system, a mandatory prerequisite is a complete analysis of the entire business system. Only the best minds within the system should be used on this phase of the project no matter how indispensable they may appear to be in their present position. Depending on the size and complexity of the organization, approximately three to ten man-years should be allocated to the analysis. It is not recommended that personnel "loaned" by computer manufacturers be utilized in this analysis, since they are likely to bias their results in favor of their own line of equipment.

Since computers provide for cross-departmental control, particular consideration must be given to the interrelationships existing among the organic functions of production, marketing, and finance since computerized systems which do not integrate decision-making, but merely perform the old jobs faster, usually do not pay their way.[33]

Operations being considered for computerized control must be clearly defined and understood. Large volumes of work must be involved and capable of being carried out, using relatively objective decision rules. Cost should be capable of being reduced especially in clerical operations. Information provided to management should be improved both in terms of its accuracy and in terms of its speed. If these qualifications cannot be met, the computer is not likely to assist in managerial control.

Everyone within the organization must be aware of what is taking place and what objectives are being sought through automated control. From top management to the operating levels, personnel must be willing to change their way of doing things and adapt to new methods. And it is wise to plan for a computerized control system to be used in parallel with the previous system until the reliability of the former has been demonstrated.

---

[33] Withington, p. 106.

BOOKS

Anthony, Robert N., *Planning and Control System—A Framework for Analysis*. Boston: Graduate School of Business Administration, Harvard University, 1965.

Awad, E. M., *Business Data Processing*. Englewood Cliffs, New Jersey: Prentice-Hall, Inc., 1965.

Barnes, R. M., *Motion and Time Study*. New York: John Wiley and Sons, 1963.

Beer, Stafford, *Cybernetics and Management*. New York: John Wiley and Sons, 1959.

Bonini, Charles P., Robert K. Jaedick, and Harvey M. Wagner, *Management Controls*. New York: McGraw-Hill Book Company, 1964.

Brooks, F. P., and K. E. Iverson, *Automatic Data Processing*. New York: John Wiley and Sons, 1963.

Buchan, J., *Scientific Inventory Management*. Englewood Cliffs, New Jersey: Prentice-Hall, Inc., 1963.

Carson, G. B., *Production Handbook*, 2d ed. New York: Ronald Press, 1958.

Clough, D. J., *Concepts in Management Science*. Englewood Cliffs, New Jersey: Prentice-Hall, Inc., 1963.

Dearden, J., and F. McFarlan, *Management Information Systems*. Homewood, Illinois: Richard D. Irwin Co., 1966.

Desmonde, W. H., *Real-Time Data Processing Systems: Introductory Concepts*. Englewood Cliffs, New Jersey: Prentice-Hall, Inc., 1964.

Downie, N. M., and R. W. Heath, *Basic Statistical Methods*. New York: Harper & Row, Publishers, 1965.

Forrester, J. W., *Industrial Dynamics*. New York: John Wiley and Sons, 1961.

Gallagher, J. D., *Management Information Systems and the Compter*. New York: American Management Association Research Study No. 51, 1961.

Goddard, L. S., *Mathematical Techniques of Operational Research*. Reading, Massachusetts: Addison-Wesley, 1963.

Grant, E. L., *Statistical Quality Control*, 3d ed. New York: McGraw-Hill Book Company, 1964.

Greenberger, M., *Management and the Computer of the Future*. New York: John Wiley and Sons, 1962.

Hall, A. D., *A Methodology for Systems Engineering*. New York: D. Van Nostrand Co., 1962.

Head, R. V., *Real-Time Business Systems*. New York: Holt, Rinehart and Winston, Inc., 1964.

Hein, L. W., *The Quantitative Approach to Managerial Decisions*. Englewood Cliffs, New Jersey: Prentice-Hall, Inc., 1967.

Jerome, William T., *Executive Control—The Catalyst*. New York: John Wiley and Sons, Inc., 1961.

Learned, E. P., C. R. Christensen, K. R. Andrews, and W. D. Guth, *Business Policy*. Homewood, Illinois: Richard D. Irwin, Inc., 1965.

Lemke, B. C., and James Edwards (eds.), *Administrative Control and Executive Action*. Columbus: Charles E. Merrill Books, Inc., 1961.

Lott, R. W., *Basic Data Processing*. Englewood Cliffs, New Jersey: Prentice-Hall, Inc., 1967.

Malcolm, D. G., and A. J. Rowe, *Management Control Systems*. New York: John Wiley and Sons, 1960.

Martin, E. W., *Electronic Data Processing, An Introduction*. Homewood, Illinois: Richard D. Irwin, Inc., 1965.

Martindell, Jackson, *Manual of Excellent Managements*. New York: American Institute of Management, 1957.

Maynard, H. B., *Industrial Engineering Handbook*. New York: McGraw-Hill Book Company, 1956.

McKenny, J. L., *Simulation for Control* (Working Paper No. 91). Los Angeles, California: Western Management Science Institute, 1965.

Miller, R. W., *Schedule, Cost and Profit Control with PERT*. New York: McGraw-Hill Book Company, 1963.

Olsen, R. A., *Manufacturing Management*. Scranton, Pennsylvania: International Textbook Company, 1968.

Optner, Stanford L., *Systems Analysis for Business and Industrial Problem-Solving*. Englewood Cliffs, New Jersey: Prentice-Hall, Inc., 1965.

Parkhill, D. F., *The Challenge of the Computer Utility*. Reading, Massachusetts: Addison-Wesley, 1966.

Porter, Elias H., *Manpower Development*. New York: Harper & Row, Publishers, 1964.

Richards, Max D., and Paul S. Greenlaw, *Management Decision Making*. Homewood, Illinois: Richard D. Irwin, Inc., 1966.

Simon, Herbert, *The New Science of Management Decision*. New York: Harper & Row, Publishers, 1960.

Strong, Earl P., *The Management of Business: An Introduction*. New York: Harper & Row, Publishers, 1965.

Timms, H. L., *The Production Function in Business*. Homewood, Illinois: Richard D. Irwin, Inc., 1966.

Vancil, R. M., J. Dearden, and R. D. Anthony, *Management Control Systems*. Homewood, Illinois: Richard D. Irwin, Inc., 1965.

Wasley, R., *Business Information and Processing Systems*. Homewood, Illinois: Richard D. Irwin, Inc., 1965.

Weiner, Norbert, *The Human Use of Human Beings*. Boston, Massachusetts: Houghton Mifflin Co., 1950.

Withington, F. C., *The Use of Computers in Business Organizations*. Reading, Massachusetts: Addison-Wesley Publishing Company, 1966.

PERIODICALS

Dearden, J., "Can Management Information Systems be Automated," *Harvard Business Review,* March-April 1964.

———, "Myth of Real-time Management Information," *Harvard Business Review*, May-June 1966.

DePaula, F., "The Implications of Real-time Systems for Management Control," *The Computer Bulletin,* June 1966.

Dooley, Arch R., "Interpretations of PERT," *Harvard Business Review,* March 1964.

Drucker, Peter, "Information, Control and Management," *Proceedings of the International Management Congress.* New York: Council for International Progress in Management, Inc., 1963.

Evans, Marshall K., and L. R. Harper, "Master Plan for Information Systems," *Harvard Business Review,* January-February 1962.

Faulhaber, T. A., "A Design for Management: Creative Planning and Control Through the Biological System Analogy," *Consulting Engineer,* October 1963.

Johnson, Richard, Fremont Kast, and James Rosenweig, "Systems Theory and Management," *Management Science,* January 1964.

Karg, R., and G. Thompson, "A Heuristic Approach to Solving the Traveling Salesman Problem," *Management Science,* 10 (January 1964).

"Keeping Ahead on Real-time," *Business Week,* March 27, 1965.

Kleinmuntz, Benjamin, "Profile Analysis Revisited: A Heuristic Approach," *Journal of Counseling Psychology,* 10, 1963.

152   Selected References

Kuehn, A., and M. Hamburger, "A Heuristic Program for Locating Warehouses," *Management Science*, 9 (July 1963).

Leavitt, H., and T. Whisler, "Management in the 1980's," *Harvard Business Review*, November-December, 1958.

"Linear Responsibility Charting: Fast Way to Clear up Confusion," *Factory*, March 1963.

Malcolm, D. G., and A. J. Rowe, "Computer-Based Control Systems," *California Management Review*, vol. 3, no. 3, Spring 1961.

Manning, J. F., "Relating a Retrieval Program to Your Company Needs," *Proceedings of the International Management Congress*, 1963.

Newell, A., H. Simon, and J. Shaw, "The Processes of Creative Thinking," in *Contemporary Approaches to Creative Thinking*, eds. Gruber, Terrell, and Wertheimer. New York: Atherton Press, 1962.

O'Meara, J., "Selecting Profitable Products," in P. M. Holmes, ed., *Readings in Marketing*. Columbus, Ohio: Merrill, Inc., 1963.

Paige, Hilliard W., "How PERT-Cost Helps the General Manager," *Harvard Business Review*, November 1963.

"SABRE: A Thirty Million Dollar Application," *Fortune*, 69 (April 1964).

Slaybaugh, C. J., "Pareto's Law and Modern Management," *Price Waterhouse Review*, XI, no. 4 (Winter 1966).

Smith, R. D., "Quality Assurance in Government and Industry: A Bayesian Approach," *Journal of Industrial Engineering*, May 1966.

———, and P. S. Greenlaw, "Simulation of a Psychological Decision Process," *Management Science*, April 1967.

Systems Development Corporation Magazine, vol. 9, no. 11, November 1966.

von Bertalanfy, Ludwig, "General Systems Theory," *General Systems*, vol. 1, 1956.

Winchell, A. H., "Mechanizing Information Systems," *Automation*, October 1965.

Index

5